THE TOSHIBA BOOK OF

Microwave Cookery

ANNEMARIE ROSIER

A Martin Book

Published by Martin Books
an imprint of Woodhead-Faulkner Ltd
Fitzwilliam House, 32 Trumpington Street, Cambridge CB2 1QY

First published 1978
Reprinted with revisions 1980, 1981
Revised edition 1983

© Toshiba (UK) Limited 1983

ISBN 0 85941 213 X

Cover photograph by John Lee
Typesetting: Westholme Graphics Limited
Printed and bound in Great Britain by
The Thetford Press Ltd, Thetford, Norfolk

Foreword

The growing popularity of the 500-watt dual-power micro-wave oven has given us the opportunity to revise the *Toshiba Book of Microwave Cookery*. New recipes have been introduced and you now have a cookery book which is specifically designed to help you get the most out of a 500-watt oven.

Jay Oldknow

Home Appliance Adviser
Toshiba (UK) Ltd

Author's Preface

When I was first at my senior school, I went to visit a food exhibition and there I saw what to me was a magic box. Food put in cold came out hot in seconds – the demonstrator needed no oven gloves even when she cooked a steamed sponge pudding in a minute. Pure magic. From that moment my dreams of becoming a great singer or train driver were finished. I wanted to work with the magic box, and now, after many years of cooking with the microwave oven, I still feel as enthusiastic.

The microwave oven has changed in design and technology since I first saw it, but still remains a superb defroster of frozen foods, cooker of raw foods, and fast heater of pre-cooked items. If you enjoy cooking, this oven, with its speed and its ability to retain the flavour and colour of food, will increase your enjoyment and, for those who dislike cooking, the labour-saving benefits of microwave will be an absolute boon.

This book has been divided into two parts. The first part deals with how the oven works and how to use it to its full advantage. The second part contains recipes and timings on heating and defrosting with the oven. All of the timings have been done on a 500-watt oven but are easily convertible for other power ovens.

Before starting to cook with your oven, do read the first part of the book. The transition from conventional cooking to microwave is simple once the basic principles have been noted. Then turn to the recipes; many will be old favourites, but see how short the cooking time is, and taste the results – good fresh hot food.

Happy microwave cooking!

Annemarie Rosier

Contents

PART ONE
Introducing the Microwave Oven

Installation, Operation and Cleaning of the Oven

WHERE TO PUT THE MICROWAVE OVEN

Place the oven on a working surface or strong shelf which is at a convenient height, preferably near a 13-amp socket. As the oven creates very few smells, steam or grease in the room, there is no need for it to be near an extraction unit. If you would like the oven built into your kitchen, ask your microwave distributor, who will be able to advise you on this. Sometimes in a kitchen there is a shortage of space, so remember that the oven can be placed on a trolley and wheeled wherever it is required, even into the garden for summer meals.

Remove all the packaging from inside the oven but make sure you do not throw away the guarantee card – in fact fill it in right away and send it off.

Plug the oven into a 13-amp socket and you are ready to cook.

OPERATING THE OVEN

Never operate the oven without food or liquid inside. Microwave ovens all differ in some small details and the instructions accompanying any one model should be carefully studied.

Having connected the oven to a 13-amp socket, you should check its operation by placing a cup of water inside. Set timer to 1 minute and press 'Start' button. The oven will now be operating. At the end of the cooking period the timer will have moved back to zero position and a bell will sound. The oven will then no longer be sending energy into the cavity.

Open the door and remove the water, which should be warm. The oven cannot be operated with the oven door open. There is no need to wait for the oven to 'warm up'. It is instantly ready to use.

CLEANING THE OVEN

One of the many joys of a microwave oven is how clean the cavity stays. Because the food is generally covered in the oven there is little splashing, and as there is no direct heat the oven walls do not get as hot as in a conventional oven.

To clean the oven, wipe it out with a damp cloth after every meal. Do not use steel wool on the surface or any harsh cleaners as they may scratch the oven surface and distort the heat pattern. Stubborn marks can be removed with a mild cleanser or by boiling water in the oven where the steam will loosen them, making the oven easy to wipe clean. The tray can be washed in the kitchen sink in warm soapy water, dried and returned to the oven.

The outside casing of the oven can be wiped over with a damp cloth and polished lightly with a spray polish.

For the oven to operate at peak efficiency the cavity must be clean.

Microwave – What it is and how it works

The microwave oven is very different from a conventional cooker in both appearance and operation. In size and design it seems more like a television set; the controls are similar, too, as are some of the components used inside. In your gas or conventional electric oven, the air is heated, which cooks the outer surfaces of the food; the heat is then passed slowly into the centre of the food by conduction from molecule to molecule. By the time the centre is cooked, the outer surfaces have browned. The hot air in the oven also heats the container that holds the food and the walls of the oven. In a microwave oven the food is heated quickly outside and in. With quick-cooking items this means that the oven will be too fast to brown the outside of the food.

The food is cooked by electromagnetic waves which come into the cooking cavity at a very fast rate (2,450 million times per second). As with all waves they are reflected off the sides of the metal cavity and form a criss-cross pattern in the oven. The food absorbs the waves from all directions. These waves cause the moisture molecules in the food to vibrate, giving friction, which is heat. If you rub your hands together you are creating friction and you will feel heat; this is just what happens to the food inside the oven.

The waves will pass straight through glass, china and paper, etc., without causing friction to the molecule structure. The main type of molecule to be affected by microwaves

9

is water, and these materials contain none. As the sides of the oven are metal, which can only reflect the waves, no energy is wasted in heating anything but the food. This also means that the cooking containers and oven cavity are easy to clean, but they will get warm, even hot, by conduction of heat from the hot food.

In the diagram the main components of the microwave oven have been indicated.

1 *Lead from oven to plug.* This is plugged into a 13-amp socket, from which the power is drawn into the oven.

2 *Power pack.* This converts the voltage to that suitable to energise the magnetron.

3 *Magnetron.* This is the heart of the oven; it converts the higher voltage to microwaves, which are very short waves similar to radio and television waves.

4 *Wave guide.* The waves are directed along the wave guide from the magnetron to the cavity.

5 *Stirrer fan.* This fan at the top of the cavity is made of several blades revolving slowly. These throw the waves into different directions in the cavity giving a better distribution of the microwaves.

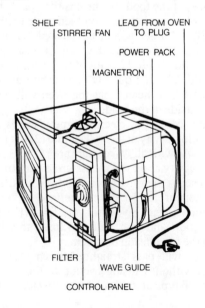

SHELF
STIRRER FAN
LEAD FROM OVEN TO PLUG
POWER PACK
MAGNETRON
FILTER
WAVE GUIDE
CONTROL PANEL

6 *Tray.* The food in the oven is raised about an inch off the floor of the oven by a glass tray to ensure absorption of the waves from all directions.

7 *Controls and door.* On the front of the oven are the controls and the door. The controls vary from oven to oven, but always include a clock which times the cooking process. The door is double-glazed for ease of cleaning with a wire mesh grill in between.

Note: All microwave ovens are fitted with an automatic cut-out which operates when the door is opened or timing ceased.

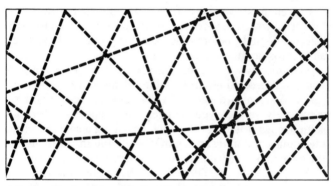

Microwaves bounce off walls of cavity and into food from all directions

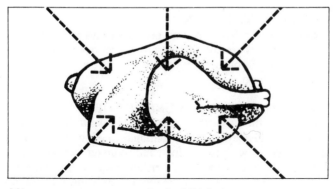

Microwaves penetrate to a depth of 1½ inches

11

Getting to Know your Oven

The microwave oven is really many appliances combined into one unit. No other piece of kitchen equipment can do so many jobs so successfully. The oven can be used for the heating of cooked food – the roast joint left over from Sunday can be served hot on Monday without drying or toughening the meat or losing any flavour. If members of your family are eating later there is no need to cook a meal when they arrive or keep food warm in the conventional oven; cook their portion with the rest and reheat as required.

Frozen food can be defrosted rapidly in the oven. No longer do you have to remember to remove the food from the freezer the night before – decide what you would like to eat and defrost in minutes in the oven.

The microwave oven can also be used for the majority of your prime cooking, from joints of meat, vegetables and cakes to scrambled eggs. On the cooking side, it will not completely replace your conventional cooker as there are some things it will not do, such as baking a soufflé, setting meringues or boiling an egg in its shell, but the many uses of the oven make it a valuable appliance in any home.

All microwave operations are controlled by time – minutes and seconds. How long the food will take in the oven is controlled by various factors, and once these have been noted the timing becomes easy.

POWER OF THE OVEN
The timings for this book have been done on a 500-watt oven, but the recipes are suitable for any power oven. The higher the watt output of the oven, the less is the cooking time that will be required.

STARTING TEMPERATURE OF THE FOOD
The colder the food, the longer it will take to be heated or cooked by the waves. In conventional cooking, generally we are concerned with frozen food and room temperature food, but with the microwave oven there are three starting temperatures – frozen, refrigerated and room or ambient. A bread roll taken from room temperature will heat in approximately 25

seconds. The same-size roll taken from the refrigerator will take approximately 30 seconds to heat up.

AMOUNT OF FOOD PLACED IN THE OVEN
There is only a set amount of energy coming into the oven cavity. When one item of food is there all the energy is absorbed into it, so, when two or more items of food are placed into the cavity, the energy is shared between them; consequently this means the food will take longer. One plated meal to heat in the oven will take 3½ minutes; two will take approximately 5½ minutes. Do not try to fill the microwave oven with food; it is quicker to heat or cook in small amounts.

SHAPE OF THE FOOD
The more even the shape of the food, the better the result. It is better to bone and roll awkward-shaped joints of meat, *e.g.* leg of lamb, before cooking in the oven. If this is not possible a thin strip of foil can be placed around the narrower ends of meat and removed halfway through the cooking time, as this will even out the cooking result.

When cooking dishes with a heavy, thick consistency in a casserole, such as cheese and potato pie, you will find that it is quite difficult to achieve a cooked centre with this sort of dish. However, if you push a tumbler, base first, into the centre of the dish, in effect producing a hollow centre to the cheese and potato pie, you will have no problem cooking it. This is because the awkward centre will have been eliminated.

DENSITY OF THE FOOD
When the food has a light, open texture it will be quicker to heat than solid items; *e.g.* a sponge pudding is quicker to heat than a steak and kidney pudding. This is because the waves can penetrate into the food more easily.

STANDING TIME
Food when removed from the oven should be left to stand for a few minutes before serving. It will not get cold because it is still cooking. The friction that is created within the food continues working and producing heat. The longer the food is in the oven, the greater the continuation of cooking on removal.

COVERS

By covering the food in the microwave oven, steam is trapped, enabling some food items to be cooked in the minimum amount of liquid, so ensuring no loss of flavour. This also helps contribute to even and slightly faster cooking. Covering a utensil will make it tend to become hot at the edges, so be careful when removing the container from the oven. Covering the food prevents splashing in the oven. Do not cover any food items that need to be kept fairly dry, *e.g.* pastry products or when cooking cakes.

The recipes in this book will show you how easily you can become familiar with all these points when using the microwave oven, so do not worry if they seem involved at the moment – remember, so did driving a car, feeding a husband or bathing a baby before you began to try.

Heating Food by Microwave

The microwave oven heats food without drying it or losing any of the colour or flavour. Cooking can be done in advance at any time, the food being left covered in the refrigerator and reheated as required. Left-overs are easily used the following day, either as part of a dish or as a meal on their own. Any canned food just requires the can being opened and the contents placed on a serving dish and heated in the oven. Members of the family can use the oven to heat their own snacks or meals if you are not there. Where there is a baby in the house, bottles can be prepared in advance and heated quickly and safely as required.

HELPFUL TIPS WHEN PLATING MEALS

If more than one serving is required, two plates can be stacked on top of each other in the oven by using a stacking ring. The top plate should be covered with another plate turned upside-down.

When plating a meal, all the food should be at the same cooked state and starting temperature. Place the food on the plate as evenly as possible. Keep the food within the well of the plate. Cover the plate during the heating cycle. Always place the thickest part of an item of food towards the edge of the plate. Gravy or meat juice should be poured over the meat

14

before heating. Leave the meal to stand covered for a few seconds before serving.

One 12 oz plated meal in the oven will take approximately 3 minutes to reheat.

TIPS FOR SUCCESSFUL REHEATING

Stir liquids, casseroles, baby food during reheating.

Empty canned foods into serving dish before reheating.

Add a little gravy to slices of meat.

Fish: put heads to tails or overlap thin parts.

Put pastry and yeast products on a rack or kitchen tissue.

Cover all foods for reheating except pastry or yeast products.

● **Remember:** Don't overtime – reheating is very quick.

Don't forget the standing time – it ensures even temperature.

If using a plate, make sure food is inside well of plate, with thinnest parts to centre.

Keep food covered when you remove it from oven.

15

REHEATING CHART

Food item	Weight	Time	Standing time
Meat/Poultry			
Chicken portion	8 oz	3½ mins	3 mins
Sliced meat with gravy	1 prtn	2½ mins	2 mins
Chops	8 oz	3 mins	3 mins
Sausages	1 lb	6 mins	3 mins
Fish			
Trout	7 oz	2 mins	2 mins
Cod steaks in sauce	4	3–4 mins	3 mins
Cod steak	1	1 min	2 mins
Fish fingers	4	1½–2 mins	2 mins
Vegetables			
Vegetables	4 oz	1½ mins	2 mins
Vegetables	8 oz	2½ mins	2 mins
Casseroles			
Chicken and mushroom	1 prtn	3 mins	2 mins
Minced beef	4 prtns	13 mins	5 mins
Steak	4 prtns	15 mins	5 mins
Pastry			
Meat pie	6 oz	2 mins	2 mins
Quiche	1 prtn	2 mins	2 mins
Quiche	4 prtns	4 mins	5 mins
Fruit pie	1 prtn	1 min	2 mins
Family-size fruit pie		3–4 mins	5 mins
Sausage roll	3 oz	50 secs	2 mins
Mince pies	6	2½ mins	5 mins
Puddings/Cakes			
Christmas pudding	1½ lb	5 mins	5 mins
Christmas pudding	1 prtn	1¼ mins	2 mins
Stewed fruit	1 lb	6 mins	3 mins
Baked apple	8 oz	1½ mins	2 mins
Sponge pudding	1 prtn	1 min	2 mins
General			
Tomatoes	14 oz can	3½–4 mins	2 mins
Sweetcorn	11½ oz can	2½ mins	2 mins
Baked beans	8 oz can	2½ mins	2 mins
Baked beans	16 oz can	3–3½ mins	3 mins
Ravioli	1 prtn	3½ mins	4 mins
Macaroni cheese	2 prtns	5 mins	4 mins

Food item	Weight	Time	Standing time
Plated meal	12 oz	4 mins	2 mins
Plated meal	16 oz	5 mins	3 mins
Soup	10 fl oz	4 mins	2 mins
Soup	1½ pts	8–9 mins	3 mins
Cook-in sauce	1 can	4 mins	2 mins
Lasagne	1 prtn	4½ mins	3 mins
Lasagne	4 prtns	15–16 mins	5 mins
Milk pudding	15 oz can	3½–4 mins	2 mins
Custard	15 oz can	3½–4 mins	2 mins
Custard	1 pt	4½–5 mins	3 mins
Bread rolls	4	1 min	1 min
Sponge pudding	10½ oz can	2 mins	2 mins
Rice	4 oz	2 mins	2 mins
Pancakes, flat	2	1 min	1 min

Defrosting Food by Microwave

The freezer and microwave oven make ideal companions – how often have you forgotten to remove the lunch from the freezer and it's been cheese on toast again, or served, because you are in a hurry, a half-defrosted cake? With the microwave oven, food defrosts quickly without any loss of flavour or problems with bacteria.

When food is frozen, ice crystals are formed inside the product; these have sharp edges and tend to reflect the micro-waves. For this reason when defrosting by microwave the oven is used in a different way – the food is placed in the oven and then subjected to a burst of waves which ensures that the ice crystals are evenly broken down.

The defrost control on your oven automatically pulses microwaves into it. To defrost items, loosen the wrapping and place the food in the oven. Set defrost control and time as given in this book or on the oven panel. Press the start button.

At the end of the cycle, remove the food. If moist, leave to stand covered before cooking or reheating. If still frozen, defrost for a longer period.

Leave food loosely covered during defrosting and stand-ing, except bakery products. Never defrost food in foil containers. Leave food standing after defrosting to even out inside temperature.

When defrosting large items, *e.g.* chicken, turn over half-way through the cycle. Mince and similar items can be separated during defrosting.

Defrost food completely before the next stage. Defrosting times are given in each recipe section, and the chart on page 20 shows additional ones together with oven speeds and required standing time.

TIPS FOR SUCCESSFUL DEFROSTING

Meat and Poultry

Remove outer wrappings before defrosting.

Place meat or poultry in the oven loosely covered, on suitable container for allotted time.

Turn joints of meat over halfway through defrost cycle.

Small cuts – chops, sausages, steaks, beefburgers, etc., are often frozen in packs of two, four or more. Place them on a rack, loosely covered. Separate as soon as possible and continue defrosting.

Packets of mince, steak and kidney, etc., can be defrosted in the covering provided. Break up as soon as possible.

Place whole birds breast down and turn over halfway through defrost cycle.

Fish

Place on large plate and cover.

Whole fish: put heads to tails.

Pieces: overlap tails or put thinner parts to centre.

Pastry

Remove wrapper and place on rack or kitchen tissue.

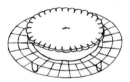

Cakes, Bread, Pastries

Place on kitchen tissue.

Standing times are quite long (follow the charts and recipes) but it's still quicker than without the microwave.

DEFROSTING CHART

Food item	Weight	Time	Standing time
Meat/Poultry			
Beef joint	1 lb	12 mins	Up to 3 lb
Lamb joint	1 lb	12 mins	in weight
Pork joint	1 lb	12 mins	20 mins
Mince	1 lb	10 mins	5 mins
Sausages	1 lb	7 mins	5 mins
Steak	6 oz	5 mins	6–8 mins
Beefburger (1)	2 oz	2 mins	2 mins
Gammon steaks	1 lb	6 mins	5 mins
Pork or lamb chops	1 lb	8 mins	10–15 mins
Chicken	1 lb	10 mins	15 mins
Chicken portions	8 oz	6 mins	10 mins
Fish			
Cod fillets	8 oz	3½–4 mins	5 mins
Haddock fillets	1 lb	7–8 mins	10 mins
Plaice fillets	1 lb	8 mins	8 mins
Trout	7 oz	6 mins	5 mins
Boil-in-bag kippers	6 oz	5 mins	5 mins
Boil-in-bag cod in sauce	5 oz	4 mins	3 mins
Cod steaks	3½ oz	2½ mins	3 mins
Puddings/Cakes			
Family sponge		3 mins	15 mins
1 individual mousse		1 min	12 mins
1 family-size fruit crumble		15 mins	10 mins
Fruit salad	14 oz	6 mins	15 mins
Strawberries	1 lb	6 mins	10 mins
Pastry			
1 Danish pastry		45 secs	5 mins
Meat pie	5 oz	2 mins	5 mins
Family-size quiche		7 mins	5 mins
Convenience Foods			
Plated meal	12 oz	5 mins	4 mins
Frozen pancakes	6	3 mins	2 mins
Family-size pizza		5 mins	5 mins
1-inch pizza		2½ mins	1 min
1 portion lasagne		8 mins	10 mins
General			
Butter	8.82 oz	2 mins	5 mins
Rice	8 oz	6 mins	5 mins
Bread rolls	4	2 mins	3 mins
Large sliced loaf		7 mins	10 mins

Cooking by Microwave

The microwave oven as a prime cooker of food has many advantages over conventional cooking methods. The time-saving element can be as much as 75 per cent on some items, but speed advantages alone would be of no consequence if the end result suffered. Food cooked in a microwave oven will have better flavour and colour retention; also the vitamin and mineral content of the food will not be lost to the same degree as when cooking conventionally.

Part Two of the book gives details of specific points to note when cooking different foods in the oven, but there are some points which relate to all foods.

PAST EXPERIENCE
Do not think of the microwave oven as a magic box and forget about the basic rules of cooking. Cooking is a science and the process of concocting and cooking a dish is done in a certain way and order for good reasons. With the microwave oven, the order of preparing a dish is not drastically altered, the ingredients only slightly, and the cooking is faster than you have been used to before. Take, for instance, a casserole – normally vegetables are sautéed, the meat sealed, then stock and seasoning added, and it is the same when using the oven. If all the ingredients were thrown into a casserole at the same time, the end result would be uneven.

TURNING THE FOOD
Most foods during their cooking cycle will be either turned or stirred. This helps the food to cook evenly and quickly in the oven. The food is not affected by opening the oven door. When a recipe says turn the food it does not mean turn it over, but turn the dish around in the oven either a quarter, third or half turn depending on the number of turns the recipe states. As you become more familiar with the oven you may find you do not need to turn the food so often, but in the beginning use the book as a guide.

LIQUID
Very often the liquid content added to a dish may be more or less than that to which you are accustomed. This is because

the microwaves react mainly on the water molecules and, to ensure good cooking, adjustments have to be made.

SEASONING
Always adjust the seasoning to taste after cooking. Because of the speed of the oven, more seasoning than usual may be needed. Do not season vegetables until they are cooked.

TIMING
If you are not sure about a cooking time, set the oven for half of your estimation, check the contents and cook for longer, if required. It is better to undercook than overcook.

CHECKING
The cooking time that is necessary can normally be judged by texture, smell, colour, etc. If it needs longer cooking, return the dish to the oven but remember the food will carry on cooking for a time after removal from the oven.

COOKING TIPS

First a few do's
and don'ts.

Don't boil eggs.

Don't deep fat fry.

Don't use batter.

Do pierce the skin
or membranes
around foods.

Meat

Don't season with salt before cooking; this dries the surface. Try one of the many proprietary brands available of seasonings or colouring.

Small cuts can be browned in a browning griddle or finished off under the grill.

Bacon will brown and crisp if cooked on a rack covered with kitchen tissue.

Larger joints – 3 lb or more – will brown during cooking but smaller ones will not. They can be finished off under the grill. Cook meat on a rack and cover loosely with split roaster bag.

Don't carve the meat until standing time is complete.

Turn joint over halfway through cooking. (Just open the door, turn the joint and close the door. Then press the cook button to re-start the power. It's completely safe and very easy.) Always use a roasting rack with a base, to catch the meat juices.

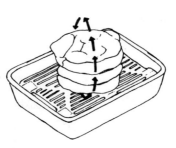

Poultry

Brush with melted fat, and sprinkle with colouring.

Cook on roaster rack with a base; cover loosely with split roaster bag.

When cooking a whole bird, start breast side down and turn halfway through cooking so that breast is uppermost.

Don't carve before standing time is complete.

Fish

Brush with melted butter.

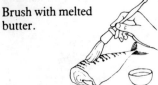

Put heads to tails or thick to thin when cooking more than one fish.

Cook covered.

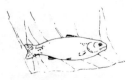

Slit skin of whole fish before cooking.

Vegetables

Add salt after cooking. Use less salt as food retains more of its flavour and goodness.

Vegetables are always cooked covered.

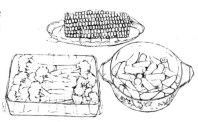

Cakes

Cakes only take minutes in a microwave!

Sponges are delicious but have a slightly different texture and paler colour.

To obtain equal rising in cakes, the dish may need to be turned more than once.

Grease cooking dish lightly but do not flour.

Dredge dish with caster sugar or put a circle of greaseproof paper in base.

Pastry

Perfect for pastry cases for quiches or flans.

Use wholemeal flour or combination of flours to get a good colour.

Don't cook choux pastry in your microwave; it's not successful.

Raw pastry items in general aren't suitable for cooking in your microwave.

COOKING CHART

Food item	Weight (approx.)	Cooking time	Standing time
Meat/Poultry			
Beef, rare	1 lb	8 mins	Joint 3 lb in
Beef, medium	1 lb	9 mins	weight approx.
Beef, well done	1 lb	11 mins	20 mins wrapped in aluminium foil
Lamb	1 lb	10 mins	5 mins/lb
Pork	1 lb	12 mins	Wrap joints
Chicken	1 lb	9 mins	over 3–3½ lb
Duck	1 lb	12 mins	in aluminium
Turkey	1 lb	9 mins	foil
Chicken portions	8 oz	5 mins	3 mins
Mince	1 lb	22 mins	10 mins
Sausages	1 lb	8 mins	5 mins
Fish			
Cod, haddock	8 oz	2½ mins	2 mins
	1 lb	5 mins	4 mins
Trout	7 oz	4–4½ mins	4 mins
Vegetables, frozen			
Peas	4 oz	3 mins	2 mins
Carrots, sliced	1 lb	17 mins	5 mins
Broccoli	8 oz	15 mins	5 mins
Corn-on-the-cob	1	6 mins	3 mins
Mixed vegetables	8 oz	8 mins	2 mins

Food item	Weight (approx.)	Cooking time	Standing time
Vegetables, fresh			
Jacket potatoes (2)	1 lb	12 mins	5 mins
Carrots	1 lb	12 mins	10 mins
Sprouts	1 lb	13 mins	5 mins
Cauliflower florets	1 lb	14 mins	10 mins

Utensils for the Microwave Oven

With the microwave oven the choice of cooking utensils is almost unlimited – because the microwaves affect only the water content of an item and very few kitchen or serving containers have water-based structures. Consequently, most non-metal containers can be used in the oven and will not be heated or damaged. In fact the waves will pass straight through them, heating only the food they hold. A certain amount of heat will of course be conducted by the food to the utensil.

Serving dishes can now be used for cooking and serving, helping to cut down the washing-up dramatically. Frozen foods can often be defrosted and heated in the plastic container in which they are purchased, or even on paper plates, serviettes and towels. There are no more burnt saucepans or awkward containers to clean when using the oven.

There is, however, one big NO – and that is to metal pots and pans in the oven. Metal reflects the waves in the oven and prevents any food from becoming heated. Over a period of time metal will also damage the oven, making dents to the cavity and ruining the heating pattern. So forget what it is like to scrub and scour pans – take a look around the kitchen and in the china and glass cupboard and meet your new cooking utensils.

CHINA
China tableware can be used throughout the day in the oven, from cooking the morning porridge in the cereal bowl to late at night when heating milk drinks in china mugs. Do not use the china if it has a gold or silver design on the plate, as 'arcing' – blue flashes of light – will occur and ruin the

pattern. Any cups or plates stuck or mended with glue should also not be used as the glue may melt.

TOUGHENED GLASS AND CERAMICS
Most Pyrex and Pyrosil containers are ideal for the oven. As with the china, the same rule applies – those with metallic edges or patterns must not be used. Most of the recipes in this book have been cooked in one or other of these types of utensil.

PAPER
Paper plates, towels and napkins can be used for heating food on. Frozen food packaged in paper containers can be used for the defrosting cycle and reheating, but if the food is raw it is not advisable to cook in this type of container as the juices from the food will make the material too wet.

PLASTIC
Plastics that cannot be broken by tearing or crushing in the hand and that are recommended for use in a dishwasher are suitable for the microwave oven. For short-term heating in the oven, freezer, picnic and storage containers are ideal. Do not heat strongly coloured foods such as baked beans in them as the colour may stain the container. Foods with a high sugar or fat content should not be overheated when using plastics, as they may cause melting. Babies' bottles can safely be heated in the oven. Any plastics designed for use as 'boil-in-the-bag' containers are ideal; prick before use. Do not use standard plastic bags in the oven as they will melt on to the food. Melamine and similar table utensils should not be used in the oven as they absorb microwaves.

GLASS
Do not use crystal glass in the oven as this contains a proportion of lead and may crack during heating; the same applies to thin-stemmed glasses. Otherwise all glass is suitable.

WOOD
Wood platters and steak plates may be used for short heating times in the oven. Avoid placing wooden items in the oven if

parts have been joined with glue; this also applies to wooden-handled pastry brushes as the bristles are held in the handle with glue.

STRAW
Straw baskets can be used in the oven for short heating times.

POTTERY
Some pottery and earthenware dishes are not suitable for use in the oven because of the type of glaze used on them. A container that heats up while the food remains cool is not suitable for microwave oven usage.

COVERS
Many of the recipes in this book recommend covering the dish. For this you can use a casserole lid, a china plate, greaseproof paper or a cooking or cling film. *Do not use* aluminium foil. Take care when removing the cover from a cooking dish as steam will be trapped beneath the plate.

Note: The container you use in the oven will affect the timing of the food. This is because it alters the shape of whatever is being heated or cooked, so be prepared when first using the oven for timings to be slightly different from those stated.

COOKING CONTAINERS

Great news – less washing up!

Serve straight from container or plate.

Don't use metal containers, dishes with gold, silver or platinum decoration, lead cut crystal, plastic containers which aren't dishwasher proof, Melamine.

There are some shapes that are better than others for microwave cookery . . .

Choose	**Avoid**	**Choose**
round dishes, shallow dishes, round soufflé dishes.	dishes with sharp corners – food gets cooked less evenly.	Pyrex, china, most plastics, glass, pottery, wood, paper – *Yes*, paper! – kitchen tissue, greaseproof paper and cling film.

Browning and Microwave

Browning of food occurs in a microwave oven when large items, *e.g.* a 3 lb joint of beef, are being cooked. This is due to the air around the meat becoming hot and the natural fats and sugars of the meat starting to caramelise, but with smaller items their time in the oven is too short for this to happen. Dishes requiring browning or crisping can be cooked in a browning dish or placed under the grill for a few minutes after cooking; this can also be done to joints of meat for a final touch.

Meat for casseroles can be coloured in a frying pan on top of the conventional cooker before being placed in the micro-wave oven. Sometimes all that is needed to complete a dish as regards colour and texture is a sprinkling of fried bread-crumbs, toasted almonds, crushed cereal or brown sugar. These can always be prepared in advance and stored in jars in the fridge or freezer and used as required.

The browning griddle can be used for browning and cook-ing smaller cuts of meat; halfway through the cooking time turn the food over.

The material used in the manufacture of the browning griddle absorbs microwave energy, similar to that of food, so the browning griddle can be preheated quite safely in the microwave oven. The surface will get very hot; add the food and it works similar to a conventional frying pan.

The griddle gets very hot, so always use oven gloves to remove it from the oven. To keep the surface of the griddle in pristine condition, use only cooking implements and scouring pads recommended for non-stick coated cooking containers.

See illustration 1 in colour section.

PART TWO
Recipes and Timings

Note: All recipes in this book serve four people unless otherwise stated.

Menu Planning

Every item cooked in the microwave oven has a preparation time, a cooking time and a standing time. Because of the short cooking times and the fact that microwave-cooked food retains its heat for a long period, it is a simple process to cook a complete meal in the oven. If any item of food should be slightly cool when it comes to be served, the dish can always be placed in the oven to boost the temperature. Use the oven when you first get it to cook just part of a meal and then progress to cooking a full meal.

HINTS FOR SUCCESSFUL MEAL COOKERY
1 Defrost food first, except for vegetables.
2 Sweets to be served cold should be cooked in advance.
3 Soups, joints or casseroles should be cooked before any vegetables.
4 The oven can be stopped at any time, the dish that is cooking being removed, another placed in the oven, and the original returned at a later time without ill effects on the food.

MENU 1

	Cooking time
Tomato soup (see page 35)	27 mins
Crispy cod (see page 57)	11 mins
Mashed potato	10 mins
Peas	5 mins
Stuffed peaches (see page 72)	8½ mins

Cook the tomato soup and divide into individual soup bowls; the soup can then be reheated as required. Cook the potatoes, season and mash. Leave in a covered serving dish. Cook the bacon topping for the fish. Cook the fish and add topping. Cover. Heat the soup. While the soup is being eaten, the peas can be cooking. The peaches can be cooking in the oven while the main course is being eaten.

MENU 2

	Cooking time
Hot grapefruit	3½ mins
Roast pork, 3 lb	30 mins
Gravy	10 mins
Bavarian red cabbage	36 mins
(see page 66)	
Potatoes	10 mins
Pineapple upside-down pudding	14½ mins
(see page 80)	

Cook the Bavarian cabbage and leave to one side. Cook the pork and cover. Cook the gravy. Cook the potatoes; place under the grill with the pork to colour and crispen. Heat the grapefruit and serve. Heat the cabbage while eating. Heat the gravy while changing plates, etc. The pineapple upside-down pudding will cook while the main course is being eaten.

When serving a large number of people at one meal, it is better to cook the vegetables in advance and heat when required, after removing the meat from the oven. Sauces should also be made in advance for large numbers and re-heated. Before starting to cook a meal it is a good idea to write down a quick time plan for the dishes and their order of cooking. After a little practice, meal planning with the oven is simple, so don't be put off.

Soups

On a cold winter's day there is nothing so warming or satisfying as a bowl of home-made soup, and in the summer one of the nicest ways to begin a meal is with a delicate chilled soup. The microwave oven produces soups so quickly that it is almost quicker to make them than to open a can or packet.

HINTS FOR SUCCESSFUL SOUPS

1 Basic stocks for soups can be made in the microwave oven by combining the required ingredients in a large casserole dish and cooking for 45 minutes. Leave to stand for 30 minutes before using.

2 Use covers for the soups only when the recipe states so.

3 Milk-based soups should be cooked in containers large enough to allow for expansion of the liquid during boiling.

4 Stir several times during the cooking of the soup, to ensure evenness of heat and a smooth end result.

5 When preparing your own recipes in the microwave oven, use slightly less fat for sautéing vegetables. Add a little more liquid than normal.

6 When adding egg or cream to a soup, be careful not to overheat.

DEFROSTING SOUPS BY MICROWAVE

When freezing soups to be reheated in the microwave oven, do not add the egg or cream. This can be added after the defrosting cycle. A pint of frozen thick soup will take about 18 minutes to defrost, thin soup about 15 minutes. Stir the soup several times during defrosting.

REHEATING SOUPS BY MICROWAVE

Stir the soup during the heating cycle. For best results heat in a straight-sided container. One pint of soup will take approximately 6 to 8 minutes to reheat, a single portion 2 to 2½ minutes. Always stir before serving.

Canned Soups

Canned soups should be removed from the tin and stirred well before heating.

Dehydrated Soups

These soups should be mixed with hot water before placing in the oven. Heat for 5 to 7 minutes and allow to stand for 10 minutes. Heat again and stir before serving.

Tomato Soup
See illustration 2 in colour section

½ oz margarine
2 rashers streaky bacon
1 small onion, chopped
1 lb tomatoes, sliced
1 teaspoon sugar
1 teaspoon paprika pepper
½ teaspoon celery salt
pinch of nutmeg
1 tablespoon instant potato mix
¼ pint water
¼ pint milk

Melt margarine in the oven for 1 minute. Add the bacon and onion; sauté for 5 minutes. Add the sliced tomatoes, seasoning and potato powder. Mix well. Pour the water over the tomatoes, cover and return to the oven for 15 minutes. Liquidise or purée the soup, add the milk and return to the oven for 6 minutes.

Cream of Corn Soup
See illustration 2 in colour section

3 rashers bacon
8 oz frozen sweetcorn
¼ pint water
1 oz margarine
1 tablespoon chopped onion
2 level tablespoons flour
1 pint milk
pepper and salt

Cook the bacon on absorbent paper in the microwave until crisp, approximately 4 minutes. Remove from the oven and cool. Cook the corn in ¼ pint of water for 6 minutes. Put to one side. Melt the fat for 1 minute, add the onion and cook for 3 minutes. Remove from the oven, add the flour, mix well and cook for 1 minute. Heat the milk for 4 minutes and slowly pour on to the flour, stirring well. Mix the corn and water into the milk. Place in the oven and cook for 11 minutes. Stir soup twice during this cycle. On removal from the oven, season to taste and garnish with crumbled bacon.

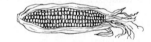

Turkey Broth

1½ oz butter
8 oz onions, finely shredded
8 oz carrots, grated
cooked meat from turkey bones
1½ pints turkey stock
bay leaf

Put butter in a casserole dish and cook for 1 minute. Add onions and carrots and cook for 8 minutes, stirring once during cycle. Purée the turkey meat with half the stock. Add this, the rest of the stock and bay leaf to the onions and carrots and cook for 20 minutes, stirring a couple of times during cycle. Leave to stand for 5 minutes covered. Remove bay leaf before serving.

Lettuce Soup
See illustration 2 in colour section

8 oz lettuce leaves
2 tablespoons water
½ oz butter
1 small onion, finely chopped
¾ pint chicken stock
½ teaspoon caster sugar
pinch of nutmeg
salt
¼ pint milk
croûtons

Place the lettuce in a covered container with 2 tablespoons water. Heat in the oven for 3 minutes. Drain and rinse the lettuce under a cold tap. Shred the leaves finely. Melt butter in the oven for 1 minute, add the onion and sauté for 3 minutes. Add the lettuce, stock and seasoning and cook in the oven for 15 minutes. Stir once during this cycle. Remove the soup from the oven and purée or liquidise. Pour the milk into the soup, check the seasoning and return to the oven for 8 minutes. Just before serving, stir and garnish with croûtons.

Onion Soup

2 fl oz vegetable oil
1 lb onions, finely sliced
½ oz flour
2 cans consommé soup
2 tablespoons dry white wine
1 teaspoon sugar
salt and pepper to taste

Put oil in a casserole dish and cook for 1 minute. Add onions, stir and cook for 8–9 minutes. Stir twice during cooking cycle. Stir in 1 oz flour, then add 2 cans consommé soup, wine, sugar, salt and pepper to taste. Cook for 14–16 minutes covered. Serve with grated cheese and croûtons.

TWO QUICK CANNED SOUP RECIPES

Celery and Mushroom Soup

1 × 10 fl oz can cream of mushroom soup
1 × 10 fl oz can cream of celery soup
2 fl oz water
1 small carton of soured cream
chopped chives

Mix the soups and water well together. Heat in the oven for 10 minutes. Stir well. Garnish with soured cream and chives just before serving.

Chicken and Almond Soup for Two

1 × 10 fl oz cream of chicken soup
½ oz butter
2 teaspoons chopped parsley
½ oz flaked almonds

Melt the butter in the oven for 1 minute. Toss the parsley and almonds in the butter and heat for 6 to 8 minutes. Stir once during this cycle. The parsley should be crisp and the almonds golden brown. Open can of chicken soup and divide contents between two soup bowls. Heat for 5 minutes in the oven. Stir and garnish with parsley and almonds just before serving.

Sauces

Sauces can be used in so many different ways, to add colour, flavour and texture to a dish, to bind ingredients together or to make a meal go further, but so often they seem a chore to make. With the microwave oven, sauces are easy to manage. They can be made in advance, being frozen or refrigerated and then heated as required, or they can be made during the cooking of a meal. You will find yourself happily adding that final gastronomic touch to the family's meal.

HINTS FOR SUCCESSFUL SAUCES

1 Good sauces need a lot of stirring to give them a smooth texture and a lovely shine, so don't be afraid to open the oven door and stir. The sauce will only be improved by so doing.

2 Try where possible to cook the sauce in the serving container as it saves on the washing-up.

3 Always cook milk-based sauces in a large container, as they tend to rise more rapidly when boiling than stock sauces.

4 Use a straight-sided container for cooking in where possible.

5 Do not cover the sauce during the cooking period unless the recipe states so.

6 Timings may vary slightly depending on the container used and the starting temperature of the ingredients.

7 If you require the sauce of a thicker consistency, cook it in the oven for a few seconds more than the time suggested.

8 Use the recipes in this section as a guideline for timings for your own favourite sauces.

DEFROSTING SAUCES BY MICROWAVE

Sauces are quicker to defrost if frozen in ice-cube trays. Add a small amount of liquid to the cubes, place in a covered container in the oven and heat for 3 minutes. Stir well and return to the oven until complete defrosting has finished.

When freezing the sauces in half-pint or pint containers, they will need between 10 and 15 minutes on defrost. Stir well to help distribute the heat during this time.

Sauces with sugar, *e.g.* apple sauce, will take about 5 minutes to be defrosted.

HEATING SAUCES BY MICROWAVE

Half a pint of thin sauce or those with sugar in will take between 1½ and 2 minutes. Half a pint of thick sauce will take 2½ to 3 minutes. Stir well before serving. Egg-based sauces should be heated slowly and the oven checked every 15 to 30 seconds.

White Sauce (coating consistency)

½ pint milk
1 oz butter
1 oz flour
seasoning

Heat the milk in the oven for 3 minutes. Melt the butter in a separate container for 1 minute. Stir the flour into the butter and cook for 2 minutes. Remove from the oven and gradually pour the milk into the flour mix, stirring well. Return to the oven for 2 minutes, stir or whisk and cook for a further 1 minute. Season to taste. Stir well before serving. Extra ingredients, *e.g.* parsley and cheese, should be added to the sauce with the seasoning and returned to the oven for a further 2 minutes.

For a thinner sauce less flour and fat should be used; for a thicker sauce increase the amounts. Timings will be altered correspondingly.

40

Curry Sauce

1 large onion, finely chopped
1 oz fat
1 level tablespoon flour
1 tablespoon curry powder
½ pint stock
2 tablespoons chutney
½ teaspoon garlic salt
pinch cayenne pepper

Place the onion with the fat in the oven for 7½ minutes. Add the flour and curry powder to the onion, mix well and cook for 3 minutes. Gradually pour in the stock, mix until smooth and cook in the oven for 3½–4 minutes. Add all other ingredients, season to taste and cook covered in the oven for 10 minutes. Stir once or twice during this cycle. Stir on removal from the oven, check seasoning and allow to stand for 10 minutes before serving. Heat as required.

Gravy

½ pint meat or vegetable stock
1 oz meat dripping
1 level tablespoon flour
1 teaspoon gravy mix
seasoning

Heat the stock for 3 minutes. Melt the dripping in the oven for 1 minute, add to it the flour and gravy mix, stir well and heat for 1 minute. Pour in the liquid stock, mix to a smooth paste and heat in the oven for 5 minutes. Stir briskly halfway through this cycle. Season as required before serving.

Apple Sauce

8 oz cooking apples
½ oz butter
sugar to taste

Peel, core and slice the apples. Place in a covered container in the oven with 1 tablespoon water. Cook in the microwave oven for 6 minutes (this timing will vary slightly with the type of apple used, but they should be soft when removed from the oven). Remove from oven and stir until smooth, add the butter and sugar, and mix well. Stand covered for 5 minutes before using.

Hollandaise Sauce

1 tablespoon water
2 tablespoons wine vinegar
4 oz butter, cubed
2 egg yolks
seasoning

Heat the water and vinegar together in the oven for 3 minutes. Stir the butter into the vinegar and beat well. Add the egg yolks and whisk until the ingredients are combined together. Heat in the oven for 1 minute and whisk in the seasoning; if not quite thick enough, return to the oven for a further minute. Stand covered for 2 minutes before serving. Care must be taken when reheating this sauce as the egg will curdle if it is boiled.

Bread Sauce

¾ pint milk
a few peppercorns
1 medium onion, peeled
2 cloves
3 oz white breadcrumbs
½ oz butter
salt

Heat the milk with the peppercorns and onion stuck with cloves for 4 minutes. Stand to one side for 20 minutes. Remove the peppercorns, add the breadcrumbs and butter, and heat in the oven for 12 minutes. Stir once during this cycle. Remove the onion, add salt to taste, stir and allow to stand before serving.

Chocolate Sauce for Ice-cream

2 oz plain dark chocolate
½ oz butter
1 tablespoon milk

Break the chocolate into a bowl with the butter. Heat in the oven for 3 minutes. Add the milk, stir until smooth and serve. This sauce can be heated gently as required.

Custard

2 tablespoons custard powder
1 tablespoon sugar
1 pint milk

Mix powder, sugar and a little milk to a smooth paste. Heat the remainder of the milk in the oven for 4 minutes. Pour on to the custard powder, stirring well. Return to the oven for 2 minutes. Stir before serving.

Egg Custard Sauce

2 large eggs
½ pint milk
1 teaspoon grated lemon rind
1 tablespoon sugar

Heat the milk and lemon rind in the oven for 2½ minutes. Whisk the eggs and sugar lightly together. Pour the milk on to the eggs, stir, strain the custard and place in the oven for 3 minutes. Whisk well twice during this cycle. Leave to stand a few minutes before serving.

Meat and Poultry

Meat cooked in the oven retains all its natural juice and flavour. The oven is easy to clean after the cooking, too. Large joints of meat will colour in the oven quite successfully, but chops, steak, etc., will need to be browned after cooking or cooked in a browning griddle.

HINTS FOR SUCCESSFUL MEAT COOKERY
1 After defrosting joints of meat in the oven, it is advisable to allow 15 mins/lb standing time before cooking.
2 For best cooking results, meat should be at room temperature rather than refrigerated.
3 Cheaper cuts of meat should be marinated before cooking.
4 Joints of meat after cooking in the oven should be allowed to stand for at least 5 mins/lb before serving.
5 Stir casseroles during the cooking cycle.
6 Turn joints of meat over during the cooking cycle.
7 If the family is divided on the degree to which meat should be cooked, cut the joint after standing time and place part back into the oven for further cooking.
8 Always cook joints and poultry on a roasting rack.
9 Turn joints around at least twice during cooking cycle.

DEFROSTING MEAT BY MICROWAVE
For even defrosting of meat it is important that the meat is as even in shape as possible. Mince, liver, kidneys, etc., should be gently separated halfway through the defrosting cycle.

Food	Time
Lamb chops, 8 oz	4 mins
Liver, 1 lb	8 mins; separate 2 mins
Mince beef, 8 oz	5 mins; separate 3 mins
Steak, 2 × 6 oz	8 mins; separate 2 mins

Food	Time
Joints of meat per lb	12 mins
Chicken per lb	10 mins

REHEATING MEAT BY MICROWAVE

Cover any meat or meat dishes to be heated in the oven. Sliced meat should be moistened with a little of the meat juices or gravy before heating. Family-size pasta dishes should be turned during the heating process. Casseroles should be stirred.

Food	Time
Lasagne, 12 oz	6 mins
Casserole, 1 portion	3 mins
Family-size casserole	15 mins
Sliced meat, 1 portion	2½ mins
Chicken, 3 lb	9 mins
Chicken portion, 9 oz	3½ mins

COOKING MEAT BY MICROWAVE

If joint unevenly shaped (*e.g.* leg of lamb), bone and roll or place strip of foil around narrow end. This prevents over-cooking of covered part. Remove foil when joint is half-cooked. Using foil will not cause damage, but ensure it does not touch oven interior.

Microwave meat thermometers can be used in the oven during cooking.

COOKING JOINTS OF MEAT AND POULTRY

Meat. Season meat and place fat side up on roasting rack. Cover with split roasting bag and cook for correct time. Wrap in foil and leave for standing time before serving.

Poultry. Season, place on roasting rack and cover with split roasting bag. Cook for correct time. Wrap in foil for standing time before serving. When cooking turkey, wrap ends of wings and legs with foil. Cook breast side down for half the cooking, turn over, remove foil and cook until time is complete. Cover with foil before serving and leave for standing time.

	Defrost	Cook	Temperature on removal from the oven
Chicken	10 mins per lb	9 mins per lb	170°F
Lamb	12 mins per lb	10 mins per lb	160°F
Pork	12 mins per lb	10 mins per lb	175°F
Beef (rare)	12 mins per lb	8 mins per lb	130°F
Beef (medium)		9 mins per lb	145°F
Beef (well done)		11 mins per lb	160°F
Turkey	12 mins per lb	9 mins per lb	170°F
Gammon		11 mins per lb	145°F

The meat or poultry can also be cooked on defrost power. This is an ideal way of cooking any meats you have which might toughen or dry by fast cooking. Cook the meat for quarter of the time suggested on full power and then double the time left and cook on defrost.

A whole chicken cooked in the microwave oven is shown in illustration 3 in the colour section.

Bacon Slices and Gammon Steaks

These can be cooked in the microwave oven. The rind of the bacon or gammon should be snipped before cooking. Place the bacon on a rack and cover with kitchen paper. An 8 oz gammon steak will take about 3 minutes to cook, two rashers of bacon about 2 to 3 minutes.

Beefburgers, Chops, Liver, Kidneys, etc.

All of these small meat items can be cooked in the oven. If browning is required then start off or finish in a frying pan or under the grill. Different seasonings can be added to give colouring, or of course use the browning griddle.

DEFROST CONTROL
In some of the following recipes defrost power is used, as it is ideal for meat cookery.

Lamb Chops

4 lamb chops
4 slices lemon
1 onion, sliced
½ green pepper, thinly sliced
½ lb tomatoes
2 fl oz stock
salt and pepper
1 teaspoon chopped parsley

Place the chops in a dish. Place the lemon slices on top of the chops. Cover with all the other ingredients. Season, cover and cook in the oven for 30 minutes on defrost, then 5 minutes on cook. Stand for 5 minutes covered before serving.

Paprika Chicken

1½ lb chicken pieces, skin removed
flour
3 teaspoons paprika
caraway seeds
¼ lb button mushrooms
½ pint chicken stock
salt and pepper
1 small carton soured cream

Toss the chicken pieces in the flour and fry in a frying pan until brown. Remove the chicken from the pan. Mix the paprika with a little water to form a thick paste. Spread this over the chicken. Place the chicken, mushrooms, stock and a few caraway seeds into a casserole dish. Cook on defrost for 25 minutes. Stir once during this cycle. Check the seasoning, and just before serving pour on the soured cream.

Cottage Pie

½ oz margarine
1 onion, chopped
12 oz cooked meat, finely minced
¼ pint stock
seasoning
1 lb mashed potatoes

Melt the margarine in the oven for 1½ minutes; sauté the onion for 3 minutes. Mix with the meat and stock. Season to taste. Place in a dish and cover with the potato. Cook in the oven for 10 minutes. Turn twice during this cycle. Place under the grill to brown before serving.

Chicken and Ham Roly-poly

½ oz margarine
2 rashers of bacon, cut into small pieces or minced
½ medium onion, minced
2 oz mushrooms, finely sliced
4 oz cooked ham (approx.), minced
4 oz cooked chicken (approx.), minced
½ teaspoon dried parsley
salt and pepper to taste
For the suet pastry:
3 oz wholemeal flour
3 oz plain flour
1 level teaspoon baking powder
½ teaspoon salt
3 oz suet
water to mix
2–3 tablespoons tomato or brown sauce

Put the margarine into a large basin and cook for about 45 seconds. Add the bacon, onion and mushrooms. Cook uncovered for 5 minutes. Stir and add the ham and chicken, parsley, salt and pepper to taste and stir. Cook for a further 2–3 minutes. Stir.
For the suet pastry: Sieve the flour, baking powder and salt into a basin. Add the suet and mix well. Add enough water to make a firm dough. Roll out the pastry into a large oval shape. Spread the chicken mixture over the pastry, leaving the edges

1 A browning griddle adds a new dimension to cooking in a
   microwave oven. This can be purchased from most large
   microwave outlets.

2 Three nutritious soups — lettuce, tomato and cream of corn

3 A roast chicken cooked in the microwave oven

4 Spicy meat loaf

5 Haddock with prawns

6 Sweet and sour prawns with rice

7 Blackcurrant flan and apple fool

8 Chocolate gâteau

clear. Brush the edges lightly with water. Spread the tomato or brown sauce over the top. Then gently roll up the pastry and filling. Pinch the side ends together. Slide pastry paddle underneath and lift on to an oval plate. Cover loosely with cling film. Cook for 3 minutes. Turn. Cook for a further 4–5 minutes. Leave to stand for 5 minutes before serving.

Savoury Mince Crumble

1 tablespoon vegetable oil
2 oz minced bacon
½ medium onion, minced
2 oz finely chopped or minced carrot
2 oz finely chopped or minced swede
½ lb minced meat
1 oz flour
1 small can baked beans
1 small can tomatoes
¼ pint hot beef stock
salt and pepper to taste
For the crumble:
2 pieces of white sliced bread
1½ oz margarine
3 oz wholemeal flour
pinch salt
1 oz grated cheese
1 oz butter

Put the oil in a casserole dish and cook for 1 minute. Add the minced bacon and onion and cook for 2 minutes. Add the carrot and swede, stir well and cook for a further 2 minutes. Stir in the minced meat and cook for 5 minutes, stirring once during this cycle. Stir in the flour, add the baked beans, tomatoes, stock, salt and pepper. Cover and cook for 4 minutes, then stir and cook for a further 5–6 minutes. Crumb the white bread, rub the margarine into the sieved flour and salt until fine, then add all but 1 oz of the breadcrumbs, add the cheese and mix well. Put the butter into a small shallow dish, cook for 45 seconds, add the remaining 1 oz breadcrumbs and mix well. Cook for 2 minutes, then stir and cook for a further 2 minutes. Put the crumble on top of the meat and garnish with the buttered breadcrumbs. Cook for approximately 6 minutes, turning once during this cycle.

Shepherd's Pie

1 tablespoon oil
1 medium onion, sliced or chopped
1 large carrot, grated
1 lb mince
4 oz mushrooms, sliced
1 oz flour
¾ pint hot beef stock
1½ tablespoons brown sauce
salt and pepper to taste
2 lb mashed potatoes

Put the oil in a 4-pint casserole dish and cook for 30 seconds.
Add the onion and carrot and cook for 5 minutes. Add the
mince and mushrooms and cook for 10–11 minutes, stirring
and breaking up the mince. Add the flour and stir well. Add
the stock, sauce, salt, pepper and peas. Stir and cover. Cook
for 20 minutes, stirring once during this cycle. Add the
mashed potato to the dish and cook for 7 minutes, turning
once. Put under the grill to finish off. If the mashed potato is
cold, heat for about 5–6 minutes in the oven before adding to
the dish.

Small Suet Meat Pudding

½ oz butter
2 rashers bacon, minced
1 small onion, minced
2 oz mushrooms, sliced
½ lb minced meat
3 oz lamb's kidney, sliced
1 tablespoon flour
¼ pint hot beef stock
salt and pepper to taste
For the suet:
6 oz plain flour
1 level teaspoon baking powder
½ teaspoon salt
3 oz suet
cold water

Grease four ¼-pint basins. Put the butter in a casserole dish and cook for 45 seconds. Add the bacon and onion and cook for 2 minutes. Add the mushrooms and the minced meat, stir well and cook for 5 minutes, stirring during this cycle to break up the mince. Add the sliced kidney and flour and stir well. Add the stock and seasoning, stir and cook for 7 minutes, stirring once during this cycle. Put the sieved flour, baking powder and salt into a bowl, add the suet and mix well. Add enough water to turn the mixture into a stiff dough. Split the dough into four, then roll out the dough and line the four basins. Use the leftover dough for the lids. Put the mince mixture into each basin, leaving about ½-inch headroom. Brush the pastry with water, put on the lids and pinch the pastry together. Make a slit on the tops and loosely cover with cling film. Put the basins spread out in the oven and cook for 5 minutes. Turn the tray 180 degrees halfway through this cycle.

Country-style Chicken and Dumplings

4 small chicken portions – remove skin
2 oz bacon, minced or chopped
1 large carrot, minced or chopped
1 medium onion, minced or chopped
4 oz mushrooms, sliced
1 oz flour
1 × 15 oz can tomatoes
¼ pint hot chicken stock
salt and pepper to taste
For the dumplings:
1½ oz shredded suet
3 oz self-raising flour
½ teaspoon mixed herbs
salt and pepper
water to mix

Joint and skin chicken. Put some oil in a large casserole dish and cook for 30 seconds. Add the bacon, carrots and onions, then stir and cook for 5 minutes. Add the mushrooms and cook for 1 minute. Add the flour and stir, then add the can of tomatoes and stir well to break them up. Make up the stock with a chicken stock cube and hot water. Add with the seasoning to the casserole, stirring well. Add the chicken joints, cover and cook for approximately 12 minutes until starting to simmer. Stir and cook for 25 minutes, stirring twice during this cycle.

For the dumplings: Mix the suet, sieved flour, mixed herbs, and salt and pepper together with enough water to make a firm dough. Divide into four equal portions in the shape of balls and add to the casserole. Cook for 5 minutes. Leave to stand for 10 minutes covered.

Note: Before cooking, the chicken joints can be browned using a browning griddle in the oven or a frying pan on the conventional stove.

Spicy Meat Loaf
See illustration 4 in colour section

4 oz chopped mushrooms
1 medium chopped onion
½ oz margarine
1 lb minced beef
1 egg
½ teaspoon salt
1 tablespoon potato powder
1 teaspoon dried parsley
1 teaspoon curry powder
1 teaspoon soy sauce
2 teaspoons Worcestershire sauce

Cook the mushrooms and onion in the margarine for 4 minutes in the oven. Drain off the fat and mix well together with all the other ingredients. Shape into a loaf on a shallow cooking dish. Cover with greaseproof paper and cook in the oven for 7 minutes.

For the sauce: Mix together 1 level tablespoon soft dark brown sugar, 1½ teaspoons mustard powder, 1 teaspoon soy sauce, 3 tablespoons chutney and 1 teaspoon curry powder. Spoon the sauce over the meat loaf and cook uncovered in the oven for a further 7–8 minutes. Leave to stand for 10 minutes before serving.

Chicken à la King

1 oz butter
3 oz mushrooms, sliced
½ green pepper, sliced
½ red pepper, sliced
1 oz flour
¾ pint milk and chicken stock, mixed
8 oz cooked chicken, diced
nutmeg
salt and pepper

Melt the butter for 1½ minutes and sauté the mushrooms and peppers for 5 minutes. Stir in the flour and mix well. Heat the stock in the oven for 4 minutes. Gradually add the stock to the flour, stirring well. Return the container to the oven for 5 minutes. Stir once during this cycle. Add the chicken and seasoning, return to the oven for 8 minutes, stir and garnish with parsley before serving.

Devilled Kidneys

1 oz margarine
1 small onion, finely chopped
salt and pepper
8 lamb's kidneys, sliced
1 tablespoon dry sherry
1 tablespoon Worcestershire sauce
1 tablespoon finely chopped parsley

Melt the margarine in the oven for 1½ minutes and sauté the onion for 3 minutes. Add the seasoning and the kidneys, cook for 2 minutes, then stir and cook for a further 3 minutes. Add the sherry, Worcestershire sauce and parsley, and cook for 3 minutes. Garnish with croûtons before serving.

Savoury Mince

½ oz butter
2 chopped carrots
1 chopped onion
4 oz chopped mushrooms
1 lb minced beef
¾ pint beef stock
2 teaspoons parsley, chopped
½ teaspoon celery salt
1 tablespoon tomato purée
1½ tablespoons porridge oats
salt and pepper

Heat the butter in the oven for 45 seconds and sauté the carrots and onions for 5 minutes. Mix in the mushrooms and the minced meat; cook for a further 5 minutes. Add all other ingredients except for the salt and pepper, cover and cook for 18 minutes. Remove from the oven and check the seasoning. Leave to stand for 10 minutes before serving.

Pork Chops with Pineapple

4 pork chops
4 pineapple rings
4 teaspoons soft brown sugar
¼ pint chicken stock
1 oz butter
5 fl oz soured cream

Season chops and colour in frying pan. Place in dish suitable for the oven, place the pineapple rings on top and sprinkle with the sugar. Pour the stock around the chops and cook covered in the oven for 4 minutes, then 8 minutes on defrost. Remove the chops and heat the liquid at full power for 5 minutes, add the soured cream and stir. Serve the chops with the sauce poured over.

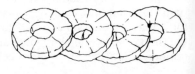

Meat Curry

2 tablespoons coconut
1 tablespoon water
1 oz margarine
1 onion, chopped
1 apple, peeled, cored and sliced
2 oz flour
1 tablespoon curry powder
¾ pint stock
12 oz cooked meat
2 oz sultanas
1 tablespoon tomato purée
½ teaspoon sugar
½ teaspoon salt
1 tablespoon lemon juice

Heat the coconut in the water for 2 minutes. Heat the margarine for 1 minute. Sauté the onion and the apple for 7 minutes. Add the flour and curry powder and mix well. Gradually add the stock and heat in the oven for 5 minutes, stirring well. Add all other ingredients, stir, cover and heat for 22 minutes. Stir once during this cycle. Stand for 5 minutes before serving.

Chicken Favourite

2 oz flaked almonds
4 slices bacon
4 chicken breasts, skinned
1 × 10½ fl oz can condensed cream of chicken soup
2 tablespoons sherry

Spread the almonds out on a 9-inch shallow dish. Heat in the oven until brown, about 8–10 minutes. Cook the bacon between layers of absorbent paper for 2 minutes in the oven. Wrap a piece of bacon around each chicken breast. Cook covered in the oven for 14–15 minutes until cooked. Drain the juices from the chicken and mix with the soup and sherry. Pour the sauce over the chicken and heat for a further 3½ minutes covered in the oven. Top with the almonds before serving.

Fish

If fish is not your favourite food to cook, try using it in the microwave oven. The first thing you will notice is that there is less 'fishy smell' around the kitchen; then you will see how firm the texture is and how good the colour, and the taste is moist and full of flavour. The dish used for cooking is so much easier to clean, too. Fish will soon become a firm favourite with you and your family.

HINTS FOR SUCCESSFUL FISH COOKERY
1 Generally fish is cooked covered.
2 Fish cooks very quickly in the microwave oven, so under-time rather than overtime.
3 Fish will carry on cooking while standing. If adding a sauce, remove the fish before completion of cooking.
4 Always brush the skin of fish with a little melted fat before cooking, as it may sometimes dry in the oven.
5 When the fish is enclosed with a skin, *e.g.* trout, make a couple of slits in the skin to let steam escape.
6 When cooking large whole fish in the oven, wrap a thin piece of foil around the tail end to prevent overcooking. Remove the foil halfway through the cooking cycle.
7 When cooking thin fillets of fish, overlap the tail ends to prevent overcooking.
8 The thickest part of the fish should be placed towards the edge of the container.

DEFROSTING FISH BY MICROWAVE
Fish defrosts very quickly in the microwave oven, as it is even in its bone structure and general composition. Keep the fish covered during defrosting and turn over once during the cycle. When defrosting prawns, etc., place in a covered container and shake at intervals.

Food	Time
Cod steak, 3½ oz	4 mins; stand before using
Prawns, 8 oz	4½ mins
Trout, 7 oz	5½ mins
Fish, 1 lb	6 mins; stand before using

HEATING FISH BY MICROWAVE

The fish that is to be heated should be kept covered except for breaded items, which should be placed on absorbent paper before being heated.

Food	Time
Portion of fish fingers	1½ mins
1 lb fried fish	3½–4 mins
1 lb fish casserole	10–12 mins

Smoked Haddock

8 oz smoked haddock
2 tablespoons milk
½ oz butter

Grease dish lightly, place the fish into it, pour over the milk and dot with butter. Cook covered in the microwave oven for 5 minutes. Remove cover and serve. This timing will alter slightly depending on the temperature and shape of the fish.

Crispy Cod

2 cod cutlets
¾ oz butter
salt and pepper
2 rashers bacon
small handful of potato crisps

Place the cod cutlets on a dish, dot with the butter and sprinkle with the seasoning. Cover and cook in the oven for 5 minutes. Remove cover and baste with the juices made during cooking. Return to the oven covered for a further 2 minutes. Remove from the oven and stand to one side covered. Cook the bacon on absorbent paper in the oven for 3–4 minutes until crisp. Crumble the bacon over the fish and sprinkle with the crushed potato crisps. If this dish is made in advance to be

57

heated later, heat uncovered so that the bacon and crisps stay firm.

Haddock with Prawns
See illustration 5 in colour section

4 pieces haddock
½ pint water
1 oz butter
1 medium onion, chopped
1 red pepper, sliced
6 oz sliced mushrooms
seasoning
4 oz prawns, peeled
1 small can sweetcorn

Skin the haddock, place the skin in the water and heat in the oven for 5 minutes. Leave to stand. Heat the butter for 1 minute and add the onion, pepper and mushrooms. Sauté in the oven for 6 minutes. Stir once during this cycle. Drain the fish skin from the water. Add the water and seasoning to the vegetables and lay the fish on top. Cover and cook for 6 minutes. Add to the fish the prawns and sweetcorn. Cover and cook for a further 3 minutes. Serve hot, garnished with parsley.

Red Mullet with Tomatoes

½ oz butter
½ medium onion, finely chopped
2 red mullets, cleaned
1 small tin tomatoes
1 teaspoon lemon juice
garlic salt
black pepper
chopped parsley

Melt the butter in the oven for 1 minute; sauté the onions in the butter for 3½ minutes. Place the fish on top of the onions and cover with the tomatoes, lemon juice and a sprinkle of garlic salt and pepper. Cover and cook for 9 minutes. Before serving, sprinkle with the chopped parsley. This dish can be served either hot or cold.

Prawn Paste

9 oz cod
8 oz prawns
8 oz butter
1 teaspoon lemon juice
½ teaspoon mace
1 teaspoon paprika
salt

Cook the cod in a covered dish for 7 minutes. Remove from the oven and pound well. Mix the prawns with the fish. Soften the butter in the oven for 3 minutes and add to the fish with the lemon juice and seasoning. Mix well and heat in the oven for 3 minutes. Put into a shallow dish and leave to set. When cool, cover with a thin layer of clarified butter and garnish with sliced stuffed olives. Leave in the refrigerator for 2 hours before serving. Serve with salad and toast or brown bread.
Note: The butter can be clarified by heating in the oven for several minutes and then straining.

Salmon Layer Crisp

1 oz butter
1 oz flour
½ pint milk including liquor from salmon
2 teaspoons lemon juice
1 egg yolk
seasoning
1 × 7½ oz can salmon
3 oz butter
5 oz breadcrumbs

Melt 1 oz butter in the oven for 1 minute. Add the flour and mix well, then return to the oven for 1 minute. Heat the milk for 3 minutes, gradually stir into the flour and mix until smooth. Return to the oven for 2 minutes. Stir in the lemon juice, egg yolk, seasoning and flaked salmon. Cook for 3 minutes. Stir and stand covered to one side. Heat the 3 oz of butter in the oven for 3 minutes. Mix in the breadcrumbs and heat for 12 minutes, stirring with a fork, until brown. Stir on removal from oven. Place a layer of the breadcrumb mix into a dish, cover with the salmon mix and top with the bread-crumbs. Heat in the oven for 4 minutes.

Sweet and Sour Prawns
See illustration 6 in colour section

2 teaspoons soy sauce
2 flat tablespoons cornflour
3 tablespoons soft dark-brown sugar
½ teaspoon ginger
1 teaspoon paprika
3 tablespoons vinegar
1 medium can pineapple pieces
2 teaspoons redcurrant jelly
4 tablespoons water
1 carrot, cut into thin strips
1 small onion, chopped
1 green pepper, thinly sliced
8 oz prawns

In a casserole dish combine the soy sauce, cornflour, sugar, ginger, paprika, vinegar, juice from the pineapple, red-currant jelly and water. Place in the oven and heat for 4 minutes. Stir well. Add the carrot, onion and peppers. Cover and cook for 7 minutes. Stir once during this cycle. Add the prawns and pineapple pieces, cover and heat for a further 6 minutes. Stir well before serving.

Fish Pie

1 lb fish
1 oz butter
1 oz flour
½ pint milk
½ teaspoon celery salt
pepper
chopped parsley
2 hard-boiled eggs
1 lb mashed potatoes

Cook the fish covered in the oven for 6 minutes. Remove and stand to one side. Melt the butter in the oven for 1 minute.

Stir in the flour and cook for 1 minute. Heat the milk for 3 minutes and gradually add to the flour, stirring well. Return to the oven for 2 minutes. Mix well. Flake the fish and add with the seasoning, parsley and chopped hard-boiled eggs to the milk. Line a dish with the mashed potatoes, pour the fish into the centre and heat for 8 minutes in the oven. Remove from the oven and place under the grill to brown just before serving.

Trout Rosé

2 medium trout, cleaned
¼ pint rosé wine
½ small onion, finely chopped
1 oz butter
2 tablespoons hollandaise sauce
salt and pepper
croûtons
parsley

Note: For the making of the hollandaise sauce, turn to the section on sauces and make this before cooking the fish.

Place trout in a shallow dish. Add the wine, sprinkle with the onions and dot with butter. Cook covered in the oven for 6–7 minutes. Remove the trout from the stock. Skin the fish carefully. Heat the stock for 4 minutes, add 3 tablespoons to the hollandaise sauce and mix well. Return the trout to the oven for 3 minutes. Add the seasoning, pour the sauce over the trout and heat for a further 2 minutes. Garnish with the croûtons and parsley.

Spicy Trout

4 frozen trout, approx. 7 oz each
2 oz butter
1 tablespoon spring onions, finely chopped
1 heaped teaspoon chopped parsley
1 large lemon
4 oz packet dry roasted peanuts

Defrost the trout for about 12 minutes and leave to stand for 10–15 minutes. Put the butter in the dish and cook for 45 seconds until melted; add the spring onions and parsley and cook for 3 minutes. Add the juice of the lemon and mix well. Put aluminium foil around the heads and tails of the trout, place in the dish and coat well with the melted butter mixture. Cover with cling film and cook for approximately 8 minutes. Add the nuts and cook for a further 4 minutes. Remove the foil and leave to stand covered for 5 minutes.

Creamy Tuna Fish

1 oz butter
¼ red pepper, finely chopped
1 oz flour
½ pint milk
salt and pepper
1 × 7 oz can tuna fish
12 black olives, stoned and chopped
2 teaspoons capers, rinsed and chopped

Melt the butter in the oven for 1 minute and sauté the peppers for 3 minutes. Stir in the flour and mix well. Return to the oven for 1 minute. Slowly add the milk, stirring well until smooth. Cook in the oven for 4 minutes. Stir well and add the seasoning, flaked tuna fish, olives and capers. Cook covered in the oven for 6 minutes. Stir and serve on hot toast as a snack or starter to a meal.

Vegetables

When vegetables are cooked by microwave, whether fresh or frozen, the full flavour and colour remains to be tasted and admired. Less nutritional value is lost during the cooking process also. Even reheated vegetables taste and look freshly cooked. When using canned vegetables, just open the can, drain the vegetables into a serving dish, add a knob of butter and heat covered until hot. Cooking vegetables in the oven is not always quicker than by conventional means, but the results are superior. Try for yourself and see.

HINTS FOR SUCCESSFUL VEGETABLE COOKERY

1 Always cover the vegetables during a cooking or heating cycle.

2 Do not add salt until after the vegetables are cooked, as it tends to dry the food during the cooking process.

3 Best results are achieved by keeping the vegetables even in size.

4 Most vegetables will need to be stirred in their dish once during the cooking cycle.

5 Standing time for vegetables after cooking is between 2 and 5 minutes.

6 Covered dishes of vegetables will keep hot for up to 10 minutes after removing from the oven.

7 With irregular-shaped vegetables, *e.g.* broccoli, place the thickest parts near to the edge of the dish.

8 Flat, shallow dishes are more successful than deep ones for cooking vegetables.

Note: When removing the cover or lid from a dish, take care not to be burnt by steam.

FROZEN VEGETABLES AND MICROWAVE

All frozen vegetables can be cooked straight from the frozen condition in the oven. The following timings have been given for 8 oz weight in all cases.

Vegetable	Water/Method	Cooking time
Asparagus	4 tbs	8 mins + 5 standing
Broccoli	4 tbs	8 mins + 5 standing
Beans	4 tbs	5 mins + 3 standing
Broad beans	4 tbs	8 mins + 3 standing
Cauliflower	4 tbs	8 mins + 3 standing
Carrots, whole	4 tbs	8 mins + 2 standing
Corn	2 tbs	5 mins + 2 standing
Corn-on-the-cob	Wrap in greaseproof paper	5 mins + 1 standing
Mixed veg	2 tbs	5 mins + 2 standing
Peas	½ oz butter	5 mins + 2 standing

FRESH VEGETABLES AND MICROWAVE

The timings will vary on fresh vegetables, depending on the age, size and freshness. All timings in the following table are for 8 oz weight, except in the case of potatoes (1 lb).

Vegetable	Water/Method	Cooking time
Beans	6 tbs	6–7 mins + 3 standing
Broad beans	4 tbs	8 mins + 2 standing
Beetroot	6 tbs	12 mins + 5 standing
Cabbage	2 tbs	6 mins + 5 standing
Cauliflower	6 tbs	9 mins + 3 standing
Celery	4 tbs	10–15 mins + 3 standing
Corn-on-the-cob	Wrap in greaseproof paper	4–5 mins + 2 standing
Onions, whole	No additions	4 mins + 2 standing
Potatoes, boiled (1 lb)	6 tbs	15 mins + 5 standing
Peas	4 tbs	9 mins + 3 standing
Tomatoes, halved	Dot with butter	3 mins
Mushrooms	1 oz fat	4 mins

To serve, drain the vegetables and season. Dot with butter and garnish if required.

HEATING VEGETABLES BY MICROWAVE

All vegetables to be heated in the oven should be covered.

Food	Time
Rice, 8 oz	2 mins; fork before serving
One portion of vegetables	30 secs–1 min
Four portions of vegetables	2 mins–2½ mins

Rice

8 oz long-grain patna rice
2 pints boiling water

Place the rice in a large bowl and pour over the boiling water. Cook covered in the oven for 10–13 minutes. Season and leave to stand for 5 minutes before serving.

Cauliflower Polonaise

1 medium-sized cauliflower
1 hard-boiled egg
1 oz butter
1 oz breadcrumbs
seasoning

Cook the cauliflower with 8 tablespoons of water for 14 minutes in a covered dish in the oven. Drain, season and keep covered. Chop finely the white of the egg and rub the yolk through a sieve. Melt the butter in the oven for 1 minute, toss in the breadcrumbs and cook until brown, approximately 4 minutes. Stir every minute. Garnish the cauliflower with the breadcrumbs, egg white and yolk before serving.

Stuffed Peppers

4 peppers
8 oz minced beef
1 onion, chopped
2 oz chopped mushrooms
1 tablespoon tomato purée
2 oz breadcrumbs
salt and pepper
1 teaspoon marjoram

Slice the top off the peppers and remove the inside. Place the peppers in a dish with 4 tablespoons of water and cook covered in the oven for 5 minutes. Place the minced beef in the oven and heat for 4 minutes. Stir, add the chopped onion and mushrooms, and heat for 6 minutes. Add the tomato purée, breadcrumbs, salt and pepper, and herbs. Fill the peppers, place in a dish and moisten with a little beef stock. Cook covered for 16 minutes. Stand for 5 minutes before serving.

Bavarian Red Cabbage

1 oz margarine
12 oz red cabbage, finely shredded
1 small onion, stuck with cloves
1 bay leaf
2 tablespoons lemon juice
1 tablespoon sugar
pinch of cinnamon
⅓ pint stock
1 large cooking apple, peeled and sliced
1 teaspoon cornflour

Melt the margarine in the oven for 1 minute. Toss the cabbage in the margarine. Cook covered for 10 minutes. Add the onion, bay leaf, lemon juice, sugar and cinnamon. Stir and heat covered for 7 minutes. Add the stock and apple. Cook covered for 14 minutes. Remove the onion and bay leaf, mix the cornflour with a little water and stir into the cabbage. Cook covered for a further 5 minutes. Stir before serving.

Ratatouille

2 tablespoons vegetable oil
2 medium onions, sliced
2 small aubergines, diced
2 large green peppers, sliced
1 lb courgettes, sliced
1 large can tomatoes or 1 lb skinned tomatoes
salt and pepper to taste

Put the oil into casserole dish and cook for 45 seconds. Add the onions and cook for 5 minutes. Add the aubergines, peppers and courgettes and stir. Cover and cook for 12 minutes. Add tomatoes and salt and pepper to taste. Cover and cook for 5 minutes until simmering. Stir and cook for a further 12 minutes. Leave to stand covered for 5 minutes before serving.

Mushroom Dumplings

These can be added to a chicken, beef or lamb casserole.

4 oz self-raising flour
2 oz shredded suet
1 teaspoon chopped parsley
4 oz mushrooms, chopped or finely sliced
½ teaspoon salt
black pepper
water to mix

Mix all ingredients together and add enough water to form a soft dough. Divide into 8 and form into balls and add to any casserole for the last 8–10 minutes of the cooking time.

Broad Beans in Tomato Sauce

1 tablespoon oil
1 small onion, finely chopped
1 small can tomatoes
1 teaspoon tomato purée
2 tablespoons water
¼ teaspoon sugar
salt and pepper
12 oz cooked broad beans

Melt the oil in the oven for 45 seconds, sauté the onion for 3 minutes, add all other ingredients and cook for 3½ minutes covered. Stir well and return to the oven for 1 minute uncovered. Pour over the broad beans and heat in the oven covered for 3 minutes. Stir before serving and garnish with parsley.

Stuffed Tomatoes

4 large tomatoes
1 oz butter
1 small onion, finely chopped
2 oz bacon, finely chopped
1½ oz breadcrumbs
salt and pepper

Cut the top off the tomatoes, scoop out the insides and tops. Heat the butter in the oven for 1 minute, add the onion and bacon, and sauté for 4 minutes. Add the breadcrumbs, seasoning and tomato flesh, stir and heat for 3 minutes. Fill the tomatoes and cover with the tops. Cook in the oven for 6 minutes. Stand 1 minute before serving.

Stuffed Marrow

1 small marrow
1 lb cooked savoury minced beef and veg
or 15 oz can minced beef
2 oz grated cheese
½ oz crushed crisps

Peel marrow and cut into 4 × 1½-inch thick rings. Remove seeds. Place into a round shallow serving dish. Add 3 tablespoons of water. Cover and cook for 5 minutes. Drain liquid from the rings. Fill with mince, sprinkle with grated cheese and cook for 14 minutes. Top with crisps before serving.

Baked Tomatoes

½ oz margarine
1 medium onion, finely sliced
3 oz breadcrumbs
2 oz grated cheese
½ lb sliced tomatoes
seasoning
chopped parsley
crushed cornflour

Melt the margarine in the oven for 30 seconds. Sauté the onions for 4 minutes. Mix the onions with the breadcrumbs and the cheese. Place a layer of the tomatoes in a greased dish, season lightly and cover with some of the breadcrumb mix. Carry on with the layering, finishing with the breadcrumbs. Cook covered for 6 minutes. Cover the dish with the remaining cheese and return the dish to the oven for a further 3 minutes. Sprinkle with the crushed cereal and parsley before serving.

Jacket Potato

1 medium-sized potato, approx. 6 oz
salt and pepper
butter

Clean and dry the potato, wrap in absorbent paper, place in the oven and cook for about 6½ minutes. Turn over once during the cooking cycle. Remove from the oven and wrap in aluminium foil. Leave to stand for 5 minutes. Slit the foil, open the potato, season and add a knob of butter before serving.

Cauliflower Cheese

1 medium cauliflower
1 oz butter
1 oz flour
¾ pint milk
4 oz grated cheese
salt and pepper

Remove the outer green leaves from the cauliflower and place it in a casserole dish. Add 6 tablespoons water, cover and cook for approximately 16 minutes. Leave to stand covered for 10 minutes. Put the butter in a basin and cook for 1 minute. Add the flour and stir, cook for 30 seconds and stir in ¼ pint of the cold milk until a smooth paste. Put the remaining milk in a jug and cook for 3 minutes. When hot, add slowly to the cold mixture, stirring well. Return to the oven and cook for 3 minutes, stirring once during this cycle. Add about 3 oz of the grated cheese and stir, then return to the oven and cook for approximately 2–3 minutes, stirring once during the cycle and at the end. Drain the water away from the cauliflower. Pour the cheese sauce over the cauliflower and sprinkle on the rest of the cheese. Cook for 2–3 minutes. Finish off under the grill if required.

Fruit

Fruit and microwave – my favourite combination. Fruit when cooked in the oven retains all its original flavour, colour and taste, even when cooking for a puréed state. Fruit dishes are perfect for reheating, too, so you can always prepare these in advance of requirements. Take care when adding sugar to a recipe, as generally less is required than with the conventional cooking methods.

HINTS FOR SUCCESSFUL FRUIT COOKERY
1 The timing will vary slightly depending on the variety of fruit being cooked, so do check by opening the oven door and testing. The end result will not be affected.
2 Take fruit out of the oven just before it is cooked. Standing time is part of the cooking time.
3 When preparing the fruit for cooking, even-sized pieces make for easier cooking.
4 Generally fruit should be covered during the cooking cycle. For maximum flavour most of the recipes recommend a little water being added. Keep the fruit covered during the standing cycle, too.
5 Before squeezing oranges and lemons place them in the oven for a few seconds and see how much more juice you get from them.
6 For easier peeling and skinning of fruit, place in the oven to heat slightly before starting.

DEFROSTING FRUIT BY MICROWAVE
If there are any apparent ice crystals on the outside of the fruit, brush them off before defrosting. The fruits should be rearranged halfway through the defrosting cycle, so stir

gently. Keep the fruit covered, except for strawberries, which are better defrosted uncovered.

One pound of fruit will take approximately 6 minutes to defrost. Let the fruit stand before using.

HEATING FRUIT BY MICROWAVE
When heating fruit by microwave, keep the item covered. With poached or stewed fruit, stir gently before serving.

One fruit portion will take between 45 seconds and 1 minute to heat.

JAM MAKING
Small quantities of jam can be made very successfully in the microwave oven.

TIPS
1 Use a very large container which must withstand boiling sugar
2 The container will get very hot and oven gloves will be needed to remove the container from the oven.
3 Put the fruit and sugar into the large container and heat until sugar is dissolved, stirring regularly.
4 When sugar is dissolved then bring to the boil; continue boiling for the cooking time in the recipe.
5 Follow the conventional cookery books for sterilising jars and covering.

Gooseberry Jam

1¼ lb gooseberries
2 tablespoons lemon juice
10 fl oz water
1¼ lb granulated sugar

Place the gooseberries, lemon juice and water in a large container, cover and cook for 12 minutes, then stir in the sugar until dissolved. Continue to cook uncovered for 15–20 minutes until setting point is reached. Stir every five minutes, then pour into sterilised jars. Test for setting point – put a small amount of jam on a saucer and leave to cool. Push your finger across the top of the jam. If the surface wrinkles, the jam is ready.

Stewed Fruit

1 lb sliced apples
¼ lb sugar
2 tablespoons water
lemon juice

Place all the ingredients into a shallow dish and cook covered for about 8–10 minutes. Stir once during this cycle. Allow to stand before serving.

Apple Fool
See illustration 7 in colour section

2 lb cooking apples
4 oz sugar
½ pint double cream
green colouring

Peel, core and slice the apples. Place in a covered dish with the sugar for 15 minutes. Stir twice during this cooking cycle. Allow the apples to cool on removal from the oven. Purée the apples. Whip the cream lightly and fold into the apples. Colour half the mix with green colouring and place in layers into four serving glasses. Serve chilled, garnished with angelica.

Stuffed Peaches

1 oz sponge cake crumbs
1 oz ground almonds
1 oz caster sugar
2 tablespoons medium dry sherry
3 good-sized ripe peaches
demerara sugar

Place the sponge cake crumbs, ground almonds and caster sugar in a bowl. Add the sherry and mix well. Heat the whole peaches in the oven for 1 minute, allow to cool and gently remove the skins. Cut the peaches in half, remove the stones and place in a shallow dish. Pile the stuffing into the stone cavities and sprinkle with the demerara sugar. Place in the oven uncovered and cook for 7½ minutes. Turn the dish once during this cycle. Garnish with blanched almonds and cherries. Serve hot or cold with cream.

Baked Apples

4 cooking apples, cored, total weight 2 lb
4 tablespoons demerara sugar
1 oz butter
2 tablespoons sweet cider
For the sauce:
2 level tablespoons demerara sugar
¼ pint cider
flaked almonds

Place the apples in a shallow dish, fill each with 1 tablespoon of sugar and top with ¼ oz butter. Pour the 2 tablespoons of cider into the base of the dish. Cover and cook in the oven for 7–9 minutes, depending on the type of apple. Remove the apples from the syrup. Make up the syrup to 5 fl oz with the additional cider. Heat the syrup with the sugar in the oven for 6 minutes. Stir twice carefully during this cycle. Pour the syrup over the apples and serve, garnished with the almonds.

Pears with Chocolate Sauce

3 large pears, peeled and quartered
3 tablespoons water
1 tablespoon caster sugar
vanilla essence
4 oz plain dark chocolate

Cook the pears in a covered container with the water, sugar and a few drops of vanilla essence for 7 minutes. Stir halfway through the cooking cycle. Drain the juice from the pears. Break the chocolate into the juice and heat in the oven for 1½ minutes. Stir well and pour over the pears. Heat uncovered in the oven for 2½ minutes and stir. Leave to stand uncovered for 5 minutes before serving.

Lemon Meringue Pie

2 lemons, grated and squeezed
water
2 tablespoons cornflour
2 oz butter
6 oz caster sugar
2 eggs, separated
1 biscuit crust flan

Make the lemon juice up to half a pint with the water. Blend the cornflour with the water, heat in the oven with the grated rind, butter and 3 oz of the sugar for 3 minutes, stir and return to the oven for a further 3 minutes. Stir well on removal. Allow to cool slightly and add the egg yolks, mix well, heat for 2½ minutes in the oven and pour the lemon mix into the flan case. Beat the egg whites until stiff and fold in the remaining sugar. Pile the meringue on to the lemon and place under the grill to brown. Serve hot or cold.

Rum and Pear Surprise

3 eating pears
1 tablespoon of lemon juice
2 oz marzipan
3 glacé cherries, halved
1 oz demerara sugar
1 oz butter
2 tablespoons rum

Peel the pears, cut in half and scrape out cores. Place on an oval dish and cover with lemon juice. Cut the marizpan into 6 pieces; put a piece of marzipan in each pear and half a glacé cherry on top. Put sugar, butter and rum in a basin and cook for 1–1½ minutes until just bubbling. Mix well and pour over the pears. Cover the dish with cling film. Cook for 5 minutes, turning once during cooking cycle. Leave to stand 5 minutes before serving. Serve with cream.

Chocolate and Orange Cheesecake

3 oz butter
10 oz plain chocolate digestive biscuits
8 oz cottage cheese
8 oz curd cheese
grated rind of 1 lemon
1 grade 3 egg
1 grade 3 egg yolk
2 tablespoons caster sugar
2 tablespoons cointreau
1 can mandarin oranges
2 oz plain chocolate

Melt the butter in a basin for 1 minute. Crumb the biscuits and press into a 9-inch flan or pie dish. Leave to cool in refrigerator. Sieve the cottage cheese or use a food processor or liquidiser. Add the softened curd cheese. Beat well and add the grated orange peel, beaten egg and egg yolk, caster sugar and 1 tablespoon cointreau. Beat well and pour into biscuit base. Cook for 8½–9 minutes. Turn during cooking. Leave to cool. Drain the mandarin oranges, use half the juice, add 1 tablespoon cointreau and leave the orange segments to soak in the juice. When cold, decorate with orange segments in two circles. Sprinkle grated chocolate over top and serve.

Desserts

The microwave oven certainly comes into its own when a quick sweet is needed to finish off a meal. Most of the recipes suggested can be left to cook while you are eating, or of course can be prepared in advance and heated as required. Sponge-based sweets will be paler than normal in colouring, but, if served with a sauce, look attractive and taste delicious.

HINTS FOR SUCCESSFUL DESSERTS
1   Cover suet sponge-based items with a cooking film, or top the bowl with a plate. Be careful on removing the cover as steam will have collected underneath.
2   Use a large container for milk-based sweets to guard against boiling over.
3   Remember to turn the cooking container during the cycle for an even end result.
4   Leave the desserts to stand for a few minutes before serving.

DEFROSTING FROZEN DESSERTS BY MICROWAVE
Care must be taken when defrosting sweets with jelly or cream as part of their ingredients. Increase the time by 50 per cent when defrosting more than one portion.

Food	Time
Pancakes (2)	30 secs
Mousse	1 min
Fruit trifles	30 secs
Fruit flan	1 min

HEATING DESSERTS BY MICROWAVE

Where jam or a sugary syrup is on the dessert, be careful not to overheat as the sugar content heats rapidly.

Food	Time
Pancakes (2)	1 min
Apple turnover	40 secs
Sponge pudding and custard	1 min; keep covered
Christmas pudding, mini	2 mins; keep covered
Family-size apple crumble	7 mins

Blackberry and Apple Crumble

1 lb cooking apples, peeled, cored and sliced
3 tablespoons sugar
2 tablespoons water
½ lb fresh or frozen blackberries
3 oz margarine
6 oz plain flour
pinch salt
4 oz demerara sugar

Put the sliced apple, sugar and water into a 3-pint casserole, cover and cook for 6–7 minutes; stir once during cooking. Remove from the oven and leave to stand covered for 5 minutes, then add blackberries. Rub margarine into sieved flour and salt until it resembles fine breadcrumbs. Stir in sugar. Put on top of fruit and cook uncovered for about 7 minutes; turn once during cooking.

Creamy Semolina

1 pint milk
1½ oz semolina
1 oz butter
1 oz sugar
nutmeg

Heat the milk in a large container in the oven for 8 minutes. Stir in the semolina and cook for 3 minutes. Add the butter and sugar, stir and return to the oven for 7 minutes. To serve, sprinkle with nutmeg.

Chocolate Cream Pie

3 oz butter
8 oz digestive biscuit crumbs
½ pint milk
1 oz butter
2 eggs
1 oz caster sugar
1 oz plain flour
1½ teaspoons cornflour
3 oz plain chocolate

Grease an 8-inch flan dish. Melt the 3 oz butter in the oven for 2½ minutes, stir in the biscuit crumbs and press well into the flan dish. Heat the milk and 1 oz butter in the oven for 3 minutes. Blend the eggs, sugar, flour and cornflour into a smooth paste and slowly add the milk to the egg mix. Heat for 3 minutes, stirring every 30 seconds. Remove from the oven and stir in the chocolate. Heat for a further 1 minute. Mix well on removal from the oven. Allow to cool slightly, spoon into a biscuit case and leave in the refrigerator to set. Decorate with cream before serving.

Steamed Syrup Pudding

3 tablespoons syrup
4 oz self-raising flour
2 oz suet
1 oz caster sugar
1 oz soft dark-brown sugar
1 heaped teaspoon Bird's Golden Raising Agent (or baking
    powder)
3 fl oz milk
1 grade 2 egg
1 level teaspoon vanilla essence

Grease a 2-pint basin and put the syrup in the base. Sift the flour into a bowl and add the suet, sugars and raising agent. Mix ingredients with a fork. Put the milk, egg and vanilla essence into a basin and heat well. Add the milk mixture to the dry ingredients and stir well. Spoon the mixture into the basin, cover loosely with cling film and cook for 5–5½ minutes. Remove from the oven and leave to stand for a few minutes, then remove the cling film and turn the pudding out on to a plate.

Kitsgarge

6 oz Danish butter, unsalted
9 oz icing sugar
3 oz cocoa
1 egg yolk
3 tablespoons milk
7 oz plain square biscuits

Melt the butter in the microwave oven for 2 minutes. Sift the icing sugar and cocoa into the butter. Stir well and return to the oven for 1½ minutes. Stir and cool slightly before adding the egg yolk and milk. Line a square dish with non-stick or greased paper. Pour in a thin layer of chocolate, cover with biscuits and repeat, ending with a layer of biscuits. Place in the refrigerator for 2 hours before serving. Turn out and decorate with cream and almonds.

Banana and Orange Pudding

1 oz butter
1 oz demerara sugar
grated rind of 1 orange
juice of 1 orange
3 small bananas, cut lengthways
2 tablespoons of brandy
cream

Melt the butter in an oblong dish for 45 seconds, then stir in the sugar, orange rind and orange juice. Put the bananas into the dish and coat well. Cover and cook for 3–4 minutes, turning the dish halfway through this cycle. Remove the dish from the oven. Pour brandy over the pudding and light. Serve with cream.

Pineapple Upside-down Pudding

2 oz butter
2 oz soft dark-brown sugar
1 small can pineapple rings
glacé cherries
5 oz margarine
5 oz caster sugar
2 eggs
6 oz self-raising flour
3 tablespoons pineapple juice

Heat 2 oz of butter in the oven for 1½ minutes. Brush on to the base and sides of an 8-inch round dish. Sprinkle the 2 oz of brown sugar on to the butter and press against the dish. Place the drained pineapple rings in the base of the dish and use the cherries between the rings. Cream the margarine and caster sugar together, beat in the eggs and fold in the flour and juice. Cover the pineapple with this mix. Even out and cover. Place in the oven for 13 minutes. Turn twice during this cycle. Allow to stand in cooking dish for 3 minutes before turning out. Serve hot or cold with cream or custard.

Wholemeal Pastry

1½ oz lard
1½ oz margarine
4 oz wholemeal flour
2 oz plain flour
pinch salt
1½–2 tablespoons water

Rub the fat into the flour and salt until it resembles fine breadcrumbs. Add water until the pastry forms into a ball. Roll out on a lightly floured board, then brush off excess flour and place on a well-greased 9-inch flan or pie dish. Dampen the pastry at the edge of the dish and prick the base. Put a piece of kitchen paper on the pastry, then place an 8-inch plate on top of the kitchen paper. Cook for 3½ minutes. Remove plate and paper, then cook for a further 1 minute. Leave to cool and then fill.

Syrup Tart
Using the above pastry case

8 tablespoons syrup
8 oz fresh breadcrumbs or crushed cornflakes
½ teaspoon lemon juice

Put the syrup into a basin and cook for 1–1½ minutes until warm. Stir in breadcrumbs or cornflakes and lemon juice, put into pastry case and cook for 6–7 minutes, turning once during cooking cycle.

Blackcurrant Flan
See illustration 7 in colour section

10 oz blackcurrants
4 oz caster sugar
1 baked flan in dish

Place the blackcurrants and sugar in a covered dish. Cook for 4 minutes, then stir and cook for a further 3 minutes uncovered. Cool the blackcurrants slightly, pour into the flan case and cook in the oven for a further 5 minutes. Serve hot or cold.

Cakes and Biscuits

It is surprising how often people arrive unexpectedly for tea or coffee when there is not a cake or biscuit in the house. That problem can be solved with the microwave oven, which enables cakes and biscuits to be produced in minutes. The oven is best suited for the cooking of light sponge cakes, not heavy fruit cakes. Care must be taken with the timing as cakes can easily be dried if left too long in the oven or cooking container.

HINTS FOR SUCCESSFUL CAKES

1 A variety of different-shaped cakes can be cooked in the oven as strong plastic, china and glass containers can be used. It is more convenient to use one container to bake in than two. The cake can be cut in half when cool.

Note: My favourite cake-cooking container is a round china soufflé dish which always gives perfect results.

2 Timings will vary according to the shape of the container used.

3 Always grease the container and line it with waxed paper or well-greased greaseproof paper at the base.

4 Do not cover the cakes during cooking, as they will tend to taste steamed.

5 Allow cake mix to stand for a few moments before placing in the oven.

6 Turn the dish during the cooking cycle for an even end result.

7 Test for doneness with a fine metal skewer as often the colour will not change during cooking.

8 Commercial cake mixes can be used in the oven; most are very acceptable.

DEFROSTING BY MICROWAVE

All types of cakes, bakery products and pastries can be defrosted in the oven. Care should be taken when items are filled with cream or butter icing. Place the frozen cake, etc., on to a piece of absorbent paper to defrost.

Food	Time
1 Danish pastry	45 secs
2 scones	1 min 15 secs
1 cream cake (8-inch)	1 min

Allow the food to stand for a few minutes before serving.

HEATING BY MICROWAVE

A doughnut or pastry, even a slice of cake, tastes fresher if it has been heated in the oven for just a few seconds before serving. This particularly applies to any product that has dried out since baking.

Victoria Sandwich

4 oz butter or margarine
4 oz caster sugar
2 eggs, beaten
4 oz self-raising flour
½ teaspoon baking powder
4 tablespoons warm water
vanilla essence

Cream the butter or margarine until soft, add the sugar and beat well together until light and fluffy. Add the eggs, gradually beating well after each addition. Sift the flour and baking powder and fold into the creamed mixture. Add the warm water and vanilla essence and fold in carefully. Put mixture into the greased round 7½-inch straight-sided dish with a circle of greaseproof paper in the base and cook for approximately 7 minutes. Turn at least once during the cooking cycle. Leave to stand for 5 minutes in the dish before turning out on to a cooling rack. When cold, cut in half and sandwich the two halves together with jam or butter cream. Dust the top with icing sugar.

For individual cakes: Using the above mixture, put a good

teaspoon into paper cases using two paper cases for extra thickness. Arrange six in a circle on the oven tray and cook for approximately 1½–2 minutes. After 1½ minutes remove any that are cooked and continue cooking remainder. When cool, cover with icing or butter icing.

Flapjacks

4 oz butter
3 oz soft brown sugar
4 level tablespoons golden syrup
pinch salt
8 oz rolled oats

Place the butter and sugar in a bowl and place in the oven for 1½ minutes until the butter has melted. Stir in the syrup and salt, then work in the rolled oats until completely mixed. Press the mixture into a greased 8-inch shallow dish. Cook for 6 minutes, turning once. Leave to cool in the dish and then cut into pieces.

Marmalade Cake

2 oz chopped peel
4 tablespoons water
6 oz soft brown sugar
6 oz margarine
3 eggs, separated
grated rind and juice of orange
3 level tablespoons chunky marmalade
8½ oz self-raising flour
1½ oz ground almonds

Line the base of a 7-inch soufflé dish. Grease the sides and base well. Cook the peel with 2 tablespoons water for 2½ minutes. Cream together the sugar and margarine. Gradually add the egg yolks, beating well. Stir in the peel, orange rind and juice, water and marmalade. Fold in the flour and almonds. Whisk the egg whites until stiff and gently fold into the cake mix. Turn into the baking dish and even out the top. Cook for 20 minutes in the oven, turning twice during the cooking cycle. Cool slightly and turn out of the dish. The cake may be iced or left plain. Store in an airtight container.

Chocolate Fairy Cakes

2 oz margarine
4 oz caster sugar
2 grade 3 eggs, well beaten
5 oz self-raising flour
1 oz drinking chocolate
1 good teaspoon baking powder
3 fl oz milk

Cream the margarine and caster sugar until light and fluffy. Add the well-beaten eggs one at a time. Sift the flour, drinking chocolate and baking powder and fold into the mixture; gently stir in the milk. Spoon the mixture into the baking cases, filling about one-third full. Either put baking cases into the bun pan, or put the mixture into two paper cases and place in a circle in the oven. Cook for 1 minute. Give the tray a half turn and cook for a further 1 minute. Remove from the oven and leave to stand on kitchen tissue. When cold, ice or make into butterfly cakes with butter icing.

Teatime Fingers

4 oz butter
5 oz demerara sugar
2 large eggs
3 tablespoons milk
6 oz self-raising flour
2 oz walnuts, chopped
4 oz sultanas
4 oz chocolate drops
½ teaspoon vanilla essence

Grease a dish approximately 11 in. × 7 in. Cream the butter and sugar together. Beat in the eggs and milk until smooth. Mix in the flour, walnuts, sultanas, chocolate and vanilla essence. Put the mix into a dish and even out. Allow to stand for 5 minutes before placing in the oven. Cook in the oven for 8–9 minutes or until firm. Turn twice during this cooking cycle. On removal of the dish from the oven, place under a hot grill until the surface is golden brown. Cut into fingers, allow to cool slightly and remove from dish. Store in an airtight container.

Chocolate Gâteau
See illustration 8 in colour section

8 oz butter
6 oz soft dark-brown sugar
3 oz treacle
3 oz golden syrup
4 eggs
5 oz self-raising flour
2 oz cocoa
1 oz coconut, desiccated

Line the base of a 7–7½-inch round dish and grease well. Cream the butter, sugar, treacle and syrup together. Slowly add the beaten eggs plus a tablespoon of flour. Beat well. Fold in the sifted cocoa and flour. Add the coconut. Pour the mixture into the dish. Cook in the oven for 8–9 minutes. Turn twice during this cycle. Turn the cake out to cool. When cold, split and fill with cream. Decorate the top with cream and mandarin oranges.

Chocolate Biscuits

2½ oz butter
4 oz plain flour
1 level tablespoon cocoa
3 oz caster sugar

Rub the butter into the sifted flour and cocoa, add the sugar and mix well by hand until a soft dough is formed. Grease a sheet of paper and place in the oven. Press six small teaspoons of the mixture flat on the paper, leaving space between each. Cook in the oven for 2 minutes. Turn once during this cycle. Remove from the paper when slightly cooled. Leave plain or decorate with icing when cold. The mix will do about 12 biscuits.

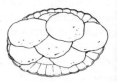

Apple Cake

3 oz margarine
6 oz self-raising flour
3 oz soft brown sugar
1 teaspoon cinnamon
1 egg
5 tablespoons milk
2 cooking apples, peeled, cored and sliced
For the topping:
1½ oz flaked almonds
1½ oz soft brown sugar
½ teaspoon cinnamon
½ oz butter

Grease and line the base of an 8-inch round, deep dish. Rub the margarine into the flour and add the sugar and cinnamon. Beat the egg and milk together and pour on to the flour slowly, mixing to a smooth batter. Add the apple slices, mix and place in the greased dish. Even out. Mix the ingredients for the topping together and sprinkle over the top of the cake. Cook in the oven for 14 minutes. Turn once during this cycle. The cake can be placed under the grill on removal from the oven to crisp the top. Allow to cool slightly before turning out from the dish.

Chocolate Truffles

3 oz plain chocolate
½ oz butter
1 teaspoon rum
1 teaspoon cream
1 oz sponge cake crumbs

Melt the chocolate in a bowl with the butter for 2–2½ minutes; stir every 30 seconds and on removal from the oven. Stir in the rum, cream and cake crumbs. Allow mixture to cool slightly, then roll into 15 individual balls. To decorate roll the truffles in drinking chocolate or chocolate vermicelli and place in small paper cases.

Microwave Florentines

2 oz butter
2 oz demerara sugar
1 tablespoon syrup
2 oz glacé cherries
3 oz walnuts
1 oz blanched whole almonds
1 oz sultanas
1 oz chopped mixed peel
1 oz plain flour

Melt the butter, sugar and syrup together in the oven for 2 minutes. Chop the cherries, walnuts, almonds and sultanas. Add with the mixed peel and flour to the melted liquid. Mix well. Place teaspoons of the mix on greased paper in the oven. Place well apart. Cook for 3 minutes, turning once. Remove from the oven and shape edges neatly with the side of a fork. When slightly cooled, lift carefully on to cooling rack. When cool, the florentines can be coated with melted chocolate on one side. Makes 12 to 15.

Miscellaneous

This section contains bits and pieces – some short recipes for the oven and a note of some of its many other uses.

Pasta and Rice

Pasta and rice can be cooked in the microwave oven. Always add boiling water to the pasta and cook uncovered in a large container. Set the oven for the time recommended on the ingredients packet. Stir and give further time as required.

The microwave oven is the only appliance which can successfully reheat pasta and rice without drying it or losing the flavour. When heating pasta, cover the container, then fork gently before serving. To heat 8 oz of rice will take approximately 2–2½ minutes; to heat 1 lb of macaroni cheese will take approximately 9–11 minutes. Defrost frozen pasta and rice dishes in covered containers. Turn during the cycle and fork gently before heating.

Pastry

Defrosting and reheating pastry items in the microwave oven is very successful, but cooking pastry items is not quite so successful. Most fillings in pies and tarts are very moist and the steam from the filling makes the pastry wet. A successful method is to cook the pastry blind, then add the pie filling and finish cooking.

Defrosting Pastry

When defrosting pre-cooked pastry items, place on a rack or kitchen tissue to absorb any moisture. Leave to stand for about 5 minutes before reheating.

Food	Time
Family-size savoury flan	6 mins + 5 standing
Family-size fruit flan	11 mins + 10 standing
Family-size meat pie	7 mins + 10 standing
Individual meat pie	3 mins + 5 standing

Reheating Pastry

When reheating pastry items, where possible, reheat on a rack and make an extra slit in the top of the pie. Always reheat uncovered. The filling inside the pie will tend to heat quicker than the pastry as it usually has a high fat or sugar content. The filling will transmit heat to the pastry; therefore when heating pastry products do not heat until the pastry feels hot, as the filling will overheat. Remove the pie when the pastry feels warm and leave to stand for a few minutes for the heat to even out. As fillings inside pies vary so tremendously, all timings are only approximate guidelines.

Cheese Scones

4 oz wholemeal flour
4 oz self-raising flour
¼ teaspoon mustard powder
½ teaspoon salt
2 good pinches cayenne pepper
2½ tablespoons baking powder
2 tablespoons parmesan cheese
1½ oz margarine
6 fl oz milk

Sieve flours, mustard, salt, cayenne pepper and baking powder. Add parmesan cheese, and rub in margarine until mixture resembles fine breadcrumbs. Make a well in the centre and add the milk. Mix in with a round-bladed knife. Roll out to ¾ inch thick and cut scones with pastry cutter. Brush off excess flour and brush the top with milk. Put a square of greaseproof paper on the tray and place 6 scones in a circle. Cook for 1½–2½ minutes. Turn over and around after 1 minute. Leave to cool, split and butter.

Scrambled Eggs

4 eggs
2 tablespoons milk
½ oz butter
salt and pepper

Beat together all of the ingredients in a glass container. Heat in the oven for 2 minutes. Stir to break up the setting egg and return to the oven for 1 minute. Stir and serve. If you require a drier egg, return the mix to the oven for a few seconds.

Poached Egg

Put two tablespoons of cold water into a small dish. Break a grade 2 egg into the dish, prick the yolk with a skewer and cook for 45 seconds to 1 minute. Leave to stand for a couple of minutes to complete cooking.

Porridge

1 cup porridge oats
1 cup milk
2 cups water
good pinch of salt

Mix all the ingredients together and place in the oven for 13 minutes. Stir twice during this cycle. For a quicker result use hot water or cook in individual bowls.

Hot Grapefruit

1 large grapefruit
1 teaspoon ground ginger
2 teaspoons brown sugar
1 teaspoon butter
2 teaspoons sherry

Cut the grapefruit in half, remove seeds and cut around segments. Place each half on a serving dish. Sprinkle with the ground ginger and sugar, dot with butter and add the sherry. Place in the oven for 3½ minutes. This will keep hot for up to 10 minutes.

Peanut Stuffing

1 small onion, finely chopped
2 oz peanuts, chopped
2 oz breadcrumbs
1 cooking apple, peeled, cored and sliced
2 teaspoons chopped parsley
1½ oz butter
salt and pepper
lemon juice
½ teaspoon dried sage

Melt the butter in the oven for 1 minute. Add the onion and peanuts and cook for 4 minutes. Add the sage, breadcrumbs, apple, parsley and 1 tablespoon water. Stir and cover. Cook for 7 minutes. Season to taste with salt, pepper and lemon juice. Use as required.

Chips and Roast Potatoes

After cutting potatoes into chips, place in the oven until warm and then fry in hot oil conventionally. This cuts down on frying time and gives a crisper chip. Blanch whole potatoes in the microwave for a few minutes before roasting.

Drying Herbs

Remove the leaves carefully from the stalks and place on a piece of absorbent paper. Put the herbs on paper into the oven and heat for 1 minute. Shake the paper gently and continue heating in 30-second periods until most of the leaves feel dry. Leave them for 2 hours before storing.

Other Handy Hints

Oven Chips and Grill Chips can be cooked in the oven. Place a 6 oz portion on a plate and heat for 3 minutes. Shake the plate and heat for a further 3 minutes, or until ready.

Butter from the refrigerator will be softened for spreading or baking by 20 seconds in the oven.

Dried apricots and prunes need not be soaked overnight. Pour boiling water over them and place in the oven for 1 minute (for approximately ½ lb). Leave them to stand for 5 minutes.

Don't scrape out jam-jars – heat in the oven and see how much more you can get from them.

When cooking fruit cakes, heat the fruit and peel in the oven with a tablespoon of water before using.

To melt chocolate, place it in a bowl in the oven and heat for 1 minute. Stir and use.

To thaw out frozen orange juice in plastic containers, remove the top of the container and heat for 3 minutes on defrost.

For quick snacks on toast, prepare the toast and heat with cheese, baked beans or tomatoes for 1 minute in the oven.

Babies' bottles can be warmed in the oven and babies' food, in suitable containers, can be heated as required.

Index